Leadership Styles
Complete Self-Assessment Guid

The guidance in this Self-Assessment is b
practices and standards in business proce ,
quality management. The guidance is also based on the professional
judgment of the individual collaborators listed in the Acknowledgments.

Notice of rights

You are licensed to use the Self-Assessment contents in your presentations and materials for internal use and customers without asking us - we are here to help.

All rights reserved for the book itself: this book may not be reproduced or transmitted in any form by any means, electronic, mechanical, photocopying, recording, or otherwise, without the prior written permission of the publisher.

The information in this book is distributed on an "As Is" basis without warranty. While every precaution has been taken in the preparation of he book, neither the author nor the publisher shall have any liability to any person or entity with respect to any loss or damage caused or alleged to be caused directly or indirectly by the instructions contained in this book or by the products described in it.

Trademarks

Many of the designations used by manufacturers and sellers to distinguish their products are claimed as trademarks. Where those designations appear in this book, and the publisher was aware of a trademark claim, the designations appear as requested by the owner of the trademark. All other product names and services identified throughout this book are used in editorial fashion only and for the benefit of such companies with no intention of infringement of the trademark. No such use, or the use of any trade name, is intended to convey endorsement or other affiliation with this book.

Copyright © by The Art of Service
http://theartofservice.com
service@theartofservice.com

Table of Contents

About The Art of Service 7

Included Resources - how to access 7
Purpose of this Self-Assessment 9
How to use the Self-Assessment 10
Leadership Styles
Scorecard Example 12

Leadership Styles
Scorecard 13

BEGINNING OF THE
SELF-ASSESSMENT: 14
CRITERION #1: RECOGNIZE 15

CRITERION #2: DEFINE: 27

CRITERION #3: MEASURE: 43

CRITERION #4: ANALYZE: 57

CRITERION #5: IMPROVE: 73

CRITERION #6: CONTROL: 89

CRITERION #7: SUSTAIN: 102
Leadership Styles and Managing Projects, Criteria for Project Managers: 128
1.0 Initiating Process Group: Leadership Styles 129

1.1 Project Charter: Leadership Styles 131

1.2 Stakeholder Register: Leadership Styles 133

1.3 Stakeholder Analysis Matrix: Leadership Styles 134

2.0 Planning Process Group: Leadership Styles			136

2.1 Project Management Plan: Leadership Styles			138

2.2 Scope Management Plan: Leadership Styles			140

2.3 Requirements Management Plan: Leadership Styles	142

2.4 Requirements Documentation: Leadership Styles		144

2.5 Requirements Traceability Matrix: Leadership Styles	146

2.6 Project Scope Statement: Leadership Styles			148

2.7 Assumption and Constraint Log: Leadership Styles	150

2.8 Work Breakdown Structure: Leadership Styles		152

2.9 WBS Dictionary: Leadership Styles				154

2.10 Schedule Management Plan: Leadership Styles		156

2.11 Activity List: Leadership Styles				158

2.12 Activity Attributes: Leadership Styles			160

2.13 Milestone List: Leadership Styles				162

2.14 Network Diagram: Leadership Styles				164

2.15 Activity Resource Requirements: Leadership Styles	166

2.16 Resource Breakdown Structure: Leadership Styles	167

2.17 Activity Duration Estimates: Leadership Styles		169

2.18 Duration Estimating Worksheet: Leadership Styles	171

2.19 Project Schedule: Leadership Styles 173

2.20 Cost Management Plan: Leadership Styles 175

2.21 Activity Cost Estimates: Leadership Styles 177

2.22 Cost Estimating Worksheet: Leadership Styles 179

2.23 Cost Baseline: Leadership Styles 181

2.24 Quality Management Plan: Leadership Styles 183

2.25 Quality Metrics: Leadership Styles 185

2.26 Process Improvement Plan: Leadership Styles 187

2.27 Responsibility Assignment Matrix: Leadership Styles 189

2.28 Roles and Responsibilities: Leadership Styles 191

2.29 Human Resource Management Plan: Leadership Styles 193

2.30 Communications Management Plan: Leadership Styles 195

2.31 Risk Management Plan: Leadership Styles 197

2.32 Risk Register: Leadership Styles 199

2.33 Probability and Impact Assessment: Leadership Styles 201

2.34 Probability and Impact Matrix: Leadership Styles 203

2.35 Risk Data Sheet: Leadership Styles 205

2.36 Procurement Management Plan: Leadership Styles 207

2.37 Source Selection Criteria: Leadership Styles	209
2.38 Stakeholder Management Plan: Leadership Styles	211
2.39 Change Management Plan: Leadership Styles	213
3.0 Executing Process Group: Leadership Styles	215
3.1 Team Member Status Report: Leadership Styles	217
3.2 Change Request: Leadership Styles	219
3.3 Change Log: Leadership Styles	221
3.4 Decision Log: Leadership Styles	223
3.5 Quality Audit: Leadership Styles	225
3.6 Team Directory: Leadership Styles	227
3.7 Team Operating Agreement: Leadership Styles	229
3.8 Team Performance Assessment: Leadership Styles	231
3.9 Team Member Performance Assessment: Leadership Styles	233
3.10 Issue Log: Leadership Styles	235
4.0 Monitoring and Controlling Process Group: Leadership Styles	237
4.1 Project Performance Report: Leadership Styles	239
4.2 Variance Analysis: Leadership Styles	241
4.3 Earned Value Status: Leadership Styles	243

4.4 Risk Audit: Leadership Styles	245
4.5 Contractor Status Report: Leadership Styles	247
4.6 Formal Acceptance: Leadership Styles	249
5.0 Closing Process Group: Leadership Styles	251
5.1 Procurement Audit: Leadership Styles	253
5.2 Contract Close-Out: Leadership Styles	256
5.3 Project or Phase Close-Out: Leadership Styles	258
5.4 Lessons Learned: Leadership Styles	260
Index	262

About The Art of Service

The Art of Service, Business Process Architects since 2000, is dedicated to helping stakeholders achieve excellence.

Defining, designing, creating, and implementing a process to solve a stakeholders challenge or meet an objective is the most valuable role… In EVERY group, company, organization and department.

Unless you're talking a one-time, single-use project, there should be a process. Whether that process is managed and implemented by humans, AI, or a combination of the two, it needs to be designed by someone with a complex enough perspective to ask the right questions.

Someone capable of asking the right questions and step back and say, 'What are we really trying to accomplish here? And is there a different way to look at it?'

With The Art of Service's Standard Requirements Self-Assessments, we empower people who can do just that — whether their title is marketer, entrepreneur, manager, salesperson, consultant, Business Process Manager, executive assistant, IT Manager, CIO etc… —they are the people who rule the future. They are people who watch the process as it happens, and ask the right questions to make the process work better.

Contact us when you need any support with this Self-Assessment and any help with templates, blue-prints and examples of standard documents you might need:

http://theartofservice.com
service@theartofservice.com

Included Resources - how to access

Included with your purchase of the book is the Leadership

Styles Self-Assessment Spreadsheet Dashboard which contains all questions and Self-Assessment areas and auto-generates insights, graphs, and project RACI planning - all with examples to get you started right away.

How? Simply send an email to
access@theartofservice.com
with this books' title in the subject to get the Leadership Styles Self Assessment Tool right away.

You will receive the following contents with New and Updated specific criteria:

- The latest quick edition of the book in PDF

- The latest complete edition of the book in PDF, which criteria correspond to the criteria in...

- The Self-Assessment Excel Dashboard, and...

- Example pre-filled Self-Assessment Excel Dashboard to get familiar with results generation

- In-depth specific Checklists covering the topic

- Project management checklists and templates to assist with implementation

INCLUDES LIFETIME SELF ASSESSMENT UPDATES

Every self assessment comes with Lifetime Updates and Lifetime Free Updated Books. Lifetime Updates is an industry-first feature which allows you to receive verified self assessment updates, ensuring you always have the most accurate information at your fingertips.

Get it now- you will be glad you did - do it now, before you forget.

Send an email to **access@theartofservice.com** with this books' title in the subject to get the Leadership Styles Self Assessment Tool right away.

Purpose of this Self-Assessment

This Self-Assessment has been developed to improve understanding of the requirements and elements of Leadership Styles, based on best practices and standards in business process architecture, design and quality management.

It is designed to allow for a rapid Self-Assessment to determine how closely existing management practices and procedures correspond to the elements of the Self-Assessment.

The criteria of requirements and elements of Leadership Styles have been rephrased in the format of a Self-Assessment questionnaire, with a seven-criterion scoring system, as explained in this document.

In this format, even with limited background knowledge of Leadership Styles, a manager can quickly review existing operations to determine how they measure up to the standards. This in turn can serve as the starting point of a 'gap analysis' to identify management tools or system elements that might usefully be implemented in the organization to help improve overall performance.

How to use the Self-Assessment

On the following pages are a series of questions to identify to what extent your Leadership Styles initiative is complete in comparison to the requirements set in standards.

To facilitate answering the questions, there is a space in front of each question to enter a score on a scale of '1' to '5'.

1 Strongly Disagree

2 Disagree

3 Neutral

4 Agree

5 Strongly Agree

Read the question and rate it with the following in front of mind:

**'In my belief,
the answer to this question is clearly defined'.**

There are two ways in which you can choose to interpret this statement;
1. how aware are you that the answer to the question is clearly defined
2. for more in-depth analysis you can choose to gather evidence and confirm the answer to the question. This obviously will take more time, most Self-Assessment users opt for the first way to interpret the question and dig deeper later on based on the outcome of the overall Self-Assessment.

A score of '1' would mean that the answer is not clear at all, where a '5' would mean the answer is crystal clear and defined. Leave emtpy when the question is not applicable or you don't want to answer it, you can skip it without affecting your score. Write your score in the space provided.

After you have responded to all the appropriate statements in each section, compute your average score for that section, using the formula provided, and round to the nearest tenth. Then transfer to the corresponding spoke in the Leadership Styles Scorecard on the second next page of the Self-Assessment.

Your completed Leadership Styles Scorecard will give you a clear presentation of which Leadership Styles areas need attention.

Leadership Styles Scorecard Example

Example of how the finalized Scorecard can look like:

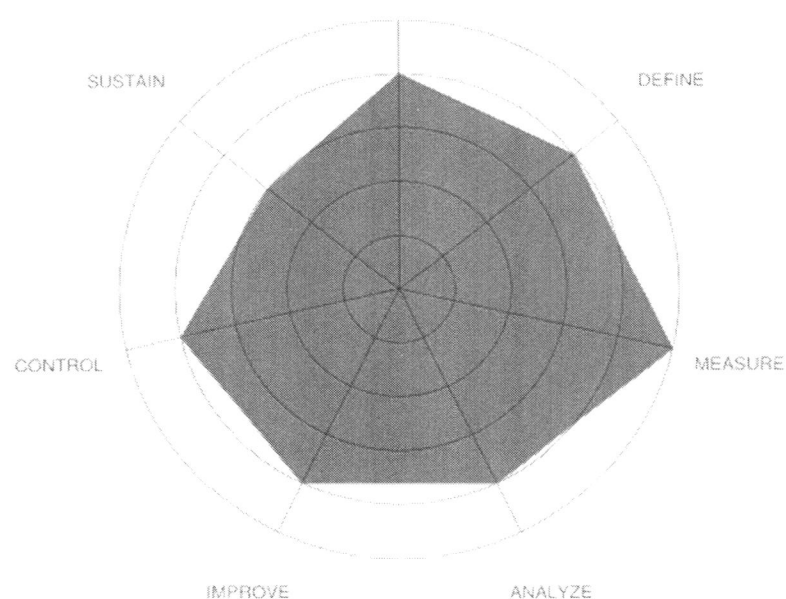

Leadership Styles Scorecard

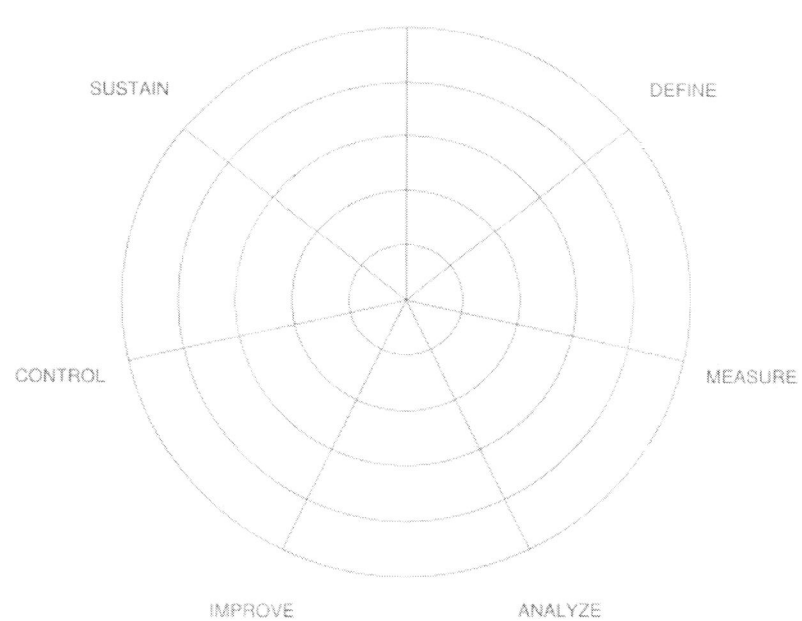

BEGINNING OF THE SELF-ASSESSMENT:

CRITERION #1: RECOGNIZE

INTENT: Be aware of the need for change. Recognize that there is an unfavorable variation, problem or symptom.

In my belief, the answer to this question is clearly defined:

5 Strongly Agree

4 Agree

3 Neutral

2 Disagree

1 Strongly Disagree

1. What are the minority interests and what amount of minority interests can be recognized?
<--- Score

2. What vendors make products that address the Leadership styles needs?
<--- Score

3. Consider your own Leadership styles project, what

types of organizational problems do you think might be causing or affecting your problem, based on the work done so far?
<--- Score

4. How do you take a forward-looking perspective in identifying Leadership styles research related to market response and models?
<--- Score

5. What prevents you from making the changes you know will make you a more effective Leadership styles leader?
<--- Score

6. Are there regulatory / compliance issues?
<--- Score

7. Who needs to know?
<--- Score

8. Are problem definition and motivation clearly presented?
<--- Score

9. For your Leadership styles project, identify and describe the business environment, is there more than one layer to the business environment?
<--- Score

10. Does Leadership styles create potential expectations in other areas that need to be recognized and considered?
<--- Score

11. How does it fit into your organizational needs and

tasks?
<--- Score

12. What situation(s) led to this Leadership styles Self Assessment?
<--- Score

13. What are the clients issues and concerns?
<--- Score

14. Where is training needed?
<--- Score

15. How do you assess your Leadership styles workforce capability and capacity needs, including skills, competencies, and staffing levels?
<--- Score

16. What are the stakeholder objectives to be achieved with Leadership styles?
<--- Score

17. Will a response program recognize when a crisis occurs and provide some level of response?
<--- Score

18. Do you recognize Leadership styles achievements?
<--- Score

19. What are the Leadership styles resources needed?
<--- Score

20. Are you dealing with any of the same issues today as yesterday? What can you do about this?
<--- Score

21. What are the timeframes required to resolve each of the issues/problems?
<--- Score

22. What do employees need in the short term?
<--- Score

23. Is the need for organizational change recognized?
<--- Score

24. Is it clear when you think of the day ahead of you what activities and tasks you need to complete?
<--- Score

25. What are your needs in relation to Leadership styles skills, labor, equipment, and markets?
<--- Score

26. Which needs are not included or involved?
<--- Score

27. How do you identify the kinds of information that you will need?
<--- Score

28. Who should resolve the Leadership styles issues?
<--- Score

29. Which issues are too important to ignore?
<--- Score

30. Are controls defined to recognize and contain problems?
<--- Score

31. To what extent does each concerned units

management team recognize Leadership styles as an effective investment?
<--- Score

32. What do you need to start doing?
<--- Score

33. What is the recognized need?
<--- Score

34. What Leadership styles events should you attend?
<--- Score

35. Did you miss any major Leadership styles issues?
<--- Score

36. What else needs to be measured?
<--- Score

37. Will new equipment/products be required to facilitate Leadership styles delivery, for example is new software needed?
<--- Score

38. What resources or support might you need?
<--- Score

39. What is the Leadership styles problem definition? What do you need to resolve?
<--- Score

40. What Leadership styles capabilities do you need?
<--- Score

41. What extra resources will you need?
<--- Score

42. Why the need?
<--- Score

43. How are the Leadership styles's objectives aligned to the group's overall stakeholder strategy?
<--- Score

44. Will it solve real problems?
<--- Score

45. Do you know what you need to know about Leadership styles?
<--- Score

46. Do you have/need 24-hour access to key personnel?
<--- Score

47. Who are your key stakeholders who need to sign off?
<--- Score

48. What is the smallest subset of the problem you can usefully solve?
<--- Score

49. Why is this needed?
<--- Score

50. What is the problem and/or vulnerability?
<--- Score

51. Why do you need Agile Leadership?
<--- Score

52. Do you need to avoid or amend any Leadership styles activities?
<--- Score

53. To what extent would your organization benefit from being recognized as a award recipient?
<--- Score

54. What would happen if Leadership styles weren't done?
<--- Score

55. Is it needed?
<--- Score

56. Are there any revenue recognition issues?
<--- Score

57. What creative shifts do you need to take?
<--- Score

58. Are losses recognized in a timely manner?
<--- Score

59. Who needs what information?
<--- Score

60. Think about the people you identified for your Leadership styles project and the project responsibilities you would assign to them, what kind of training do you think they would need to perform these responsibilities effectively?
<--- Score

61. What should be considered when identifying available resources, constraints, and deadlines?

<--- Score

62. Who else hopes to benefit from it?
<--- Score

63. Have you identified your Leadership styles key performance indicators?
<--- Score

64. What needs to be done?
<--- Score

65. Can management personnel recognize the monetary benefit of Leadership styles?
<--- Score

66. How can auditing be a preventative security measure?
<--- Score

67. Will Leadership styles deliverables need to be tested and, if so, by whom?
<--- Score

68. Would you recognize a threat from the inside?
<--- Score

69. Are employees recognized or rewarded for performance that demonstrates the highest levels of integrity?
<--- Score

70. How many trainings, in total, are needed?
<--- Score

71. Do you need different information or graphics?

<--- Score

72. How do you recognize an objection?
<--- Score

73. What are the expected benefits of Leadership styles to the stakeholder?
<--- Score

74. Are there any specific expectations or concerns about the Leadership styles team, Leadership styles itself?
<--- Score

75. What tools and technologies are needed for a custom Leadership styles project?
<--- Score

76. Is the quality assurance team identified?
<--- Score

77. What needs to stay?
<--- Score

78. What problems are you facing and how do you consider Leadership styles will circumvent those obstacles?
<--- Score

79. Who needs to know about Leadership styles?
<--- Score

80. How do you recognize an Leadership styles objection?
<--- Score

81. What is the problem or issue?
<--- Score

82. What Leadership styles problem should be solved?
<--- Score

83. What does Leadership styles success mean to the stakeholders?
<--- Score

84. Are employees recognized for desired behaviors?
<--- Score

85. Are there recognized Leadership styles problems?
<--- Score

86. Who defines the rules in relation to any given issue?
<--- Score

87. Which information does the Leadership styles business case need to include?
<--- Score

88. Are your goals realistic? Do you need to redefine your problem? Perhaps the problem has changed or maybe you have reached your goal and need to set a new one?
<--- Score

89. What information do users need?
<--- Score

90. How are you going to measure success?
<--- Score

91. Does the problem have ethical dimensions?
<--- Score

92. How are training requirements identified?
<--- Score

93. What training and capacity building actions are needed to implement proposed reforms?
<--- Score

94. Where do you need to exercise leadership?
<--- Score

95. Are there Leadership styles problems defined?
<--- Score

96. What activities does the governance board need to consider?
<--- Score

97. When a Leadership styles manager recognizes a problem, what options are available?
<--- Score

98. How much are sponsors, customers, partners, stakeholders involved in Leadership styles? In other words, what are the risks, if Leadership styles does not deliver successfully?
<--- Score

99. As a sponsor, customer or management, how important is it to meet goals, objectives?
<--- Score

100. What Leadership styles coordination do you need?

<--- Score

Add up total points for this section:
_____ = Total points for this section

Divided by: _____ (number of statements answered) = _____
Average score for this section

Transfer your score to the Leadership styles Index at the beginning of the Self-Assessment.

CRITERION #2: DEFINE:

INTENT: Formulate the stakeholder problem. Define the problem, needs and objectives.

In my belief, the answer to this question is clearly defined:

5 Strongly Agree

4 Agree

3 Neutral

2 Disagree

1 Strongly Disagree

1. What sort of initial information to gather?
<--- Score

2. Is there a completed, verified, and validated high-level 'as is' (not 'should be' or 'could be') stakeholder process map?
<--- Score

3. When is/was the Leadership styles start date?

<--- Score

4. What is the scope of Leadership styles?
<--- Score

5. Is special Leadership styles user knowledge required?
<--- Score

6. Who approved the Leadership styles scope?
<--- Score

7. Have all of the relationships been defined properly?
<--- Score

8. What is a worst-case scenario for losses?
<--- Score

9. Are accountability and ownership for Leadership styles clearly defined?
<--- Score

10. What knowledge or experience is required?
<--- Score

11. What is out of scope?
<--- Score

12. When is the estimated completion date?
<--- Score

13. Have the customer needs been translated into specific, measurable requirements? How?
<--- Score

14. Does the team have regular meetings?

<--- Score

15. How do you gather requirements?
<--- Score

16. When are meeting minutes sent out? Who is on the distribution list?
<--- Score

17. What constraints exist that might impact the team?
<--- Score

18. How and when will the baselines be defined?
<--- Score

19. Does the scope remain the same?
<--- Score

20. Will team members perform Leadership styles work when assigned and in a timely fashion?
<--- Score

21. What are the compelling stakeholder reasons for embarking on Leadership styles?
<--- Score

22. Is the current 'as is' process being followed? If not, what are the discrepancies?
<--- Score

23. What customer feedback methods were used to solicit their input?
<--- Score

24. Are audit criteria, scope, frequency and methods

defined?
<--- Score

25. Are the Leadership styles requirements complete?
<--- Score

26. Is the improvement team aware of the different versions of a process: what they think it is vs. what it actually is vs. what it should be vs. what it could be?
<--- Score

27. What is the scope?
<--- Score

28. What information do you gather?
<--- Score

29. Is there regularly 100% attendance at the team meetings? If not, have appointed substitutes attended to preserve cross-functionality and full representation?
<--- Score

30. What information should you gather?
<--- Score

31. Has a high-level 'as is' process map been completed, verified and validated?
<--- Score

32. Is there a completed SIPOC representation, describing the Suppliers, Inputs, Process, Outputs, and Customers?
<--- Score

33. In what way can you redefine the criteria of choice

clients have in your category in your favor?
<--- Score

34. Who is gathering information?
<--- Score

35. What scope to assess?
<--- Score

36. How will the Leadership styles team and the group measure complete success of Leadership styles?
<--- Score

37. How do you build the right business case?
<--- Score

38. Has your scope been defined?
<--- Score

39. Who are the Leadership styles improvement team members, including Management Leads and Coaches?
<--- Score

40. Have specific policy objectives been defined?
<--- Score

41. Is full participation by members in regularly held team meetings guaranteed?
<--- Score

42. Are roles and responsibilities formally defined?
<--- Score

43. How do you think the partners involved in Leadership styles would have defined success?

<--- Score

44. Has the Leadership styles work been fairly and/or equitably divided and delegated among team members who are qualified and capable to perform the work? Has everyone contributed?
<--- Score

45. Are the Leadership styles requirements testable?
<--- Score

46. What is in the scope and what is not in scope?
<--- Score

47. What system do you use for gathering Leadership styles information?
<--- Score

48. What is the scope of the Leadership styles effort?
<--- Score

49. What defines best in class?
<--- Score

50. Has everyone on the team, including the team leaders, been properly trained?
<--- Score

51. Has a project plan, Gantt chart, or similar been developed/completed?
<--- Score

52. Is the work to date meeting requirements?
<--- Score

53. What specifically is the problem? Where does it

occur? When does it occur? What is its extent?
<--- Score

54. Who defines (or who defined) the rules and roles?
<--- Score

55. Is there any additional Leadership styles definition of success?
<--- Score

56. How do you manage scope?
<--- Score

57. Has the improvement team collected the 'voice of the customer' (obtained feedback – qualitative and quantitative)?
<--- Score

58. What are the dynamics of the communication plan?
<--- Score

59. Is there a Leadership styles management charter, including stakeholder case, problem and goal statements, scope, milestones, roles and responsibilities, communication plan?
<--- Score

60. Is the scope of Leadership styles defined?
<--- Score

61. What Leadership styles requirements should be gathered?
<--- Score

62. What are the boundaries of the scope? What is in

bounds and what is not? What is the start point? What is the stop point?
<--- Score

63. How was the 'as is' process map developed, reviewed, verified and validated?
<--- Score

64. Is the Leadership styles scope complete and appropriately sized?
<--- Score

65. What sources do you use to gather information for a Leadership styles study?
<--- Score

66. Do you all define Leadership styles in the same way?
<--- Score

67. What are the Leadership styles tasks and definitions?
<--- Score

68. Will a Leadership styles production readiness review be required?
<--- Score

69. Do the problem and goal statements meet the SMART criteria (specific, measurable, attainable, relevant, and time-bound)?
<--- Score

70. How will variation in the actual durations of each activity be dealt with to ensure that the expected Leadership styles results are met?

<--- Score

71. Are all requirements met?
<--- Score

72. Has anyone else (internal or external to the group) attempted to solve this problem or a similar one before? If so, what knowledge can be leveraged from these previous efforts?
<--- Score

73. Why are you doing Leadership styles and what is the scope?
<--- Score

74. What is the worst case scenario?
<--- Score

75. Do you have organizational privacy requirements?
<--- Score

76. How is the team tracking and documenting its work?
<--- Score

77. Has the direction changed at all during the course of Leadership styles? If so, when did it change and why?
<--- Score

78. What is the scope of the Leadership styles work?
<--- Score

79. What is out-of-scope initially?
<--- Score

80. How do you gather the stories?
<--- Score

81. How do you manage unclear Leadership styles requirements?
<--- Score

82. What are the tasks and definitions?
<--- Score

83. Is it clearly defined in and to your organization what you do?
<--- Score

84. How did the Leadership styles manager receive input to the development of a Leadership styles improvement plan and the estimated completion dates/times of each activity?
<--- Score

85. Is there a clear Leadership styles case definition?
<--- Score

86. Is there a critical path to deliver Leadership styles results?
<--- Score

87. How often are the team meetings?
<--- Score

88. Are required metrics defined, what are they?
<--- Score

89. What intelligence can you gather?
<--- Score

90. Where can you gather more information?
<--- Score

91. What was the context?
<--- Score

92. Are different versions of process maps needed to account for the different types of inputs?
<--- Score

93. How do you catch Leadership styles definition inconsistencies?
<--- Score

94. Are there any constraints known that bear on the ability to perform Leadership styles work? How is the team addressing them?
<--- Score

95. Has/have the customer(s) been identified?
<--- Score

96. What are the requirements for audit information?
<--- Score

97. How do you hand over Leadership styles context?
<--- Score

98. What is the definition of success?
<--- Score

99. What would be the goal or target for a Leadership styles's improvement team?
<--- Score

100. How do you gather Leadership styles

requirements?
<--- Score

101. What critical content must be communicated – who, what, when, where, and how?
<--- Score

102. Has a Leadership styles requirement not been met?
<--- Score

103. Are there different segments of customers?
<--- Score

104. Who is gathering Leadership styles information?
<--- Score

105. What are the record-keeping requirements of Leadership styles activities?
<--- Score

106. What key stakeholder process output measure(s) does Leadership styles leverage and how?
<--- Score

107. Has a team charter been developed and communicated?
<--- Score

108. Are resources adequate for the scope?
<--- Score

109. Have all basic functions of Leadership styles been defined?
<--- Score

110. What are the core elements of the Leadership styles business case?
<--- Score

111. Is scope creep really all bad news?
<--- Score

112. What are the rough order estimates on cost savings/opportunities that Leadership styles brings?
<--- Score

113. How are consistent Leadership styles definitions important?
<--- Score

114. What are the Leadership styles use cases?
<--- Score

115. Is the team equipped with available and reliable resources?
<--- Score

116. Are customer(s) identified and segmented according to their different needs and requirements?
<--- Score

117. What baselines are required to be defined and managed?
<--- Score

118. How have you defined all Leadership styles requirements first?
<--- Score

119. Are approval levels defined for contracts and supplements to contracts?

<--- Score

120. How do you keep key subject matter experts in the loop?
<--- Score

121. Will team members regularly document their Leadership styles work?
<--- Score

122. What scope do you want your strategy to cover?
<--- Score

123. What is the context?
<--- Score

124. What are the Roles and Responsibilities for each team member and its leadership? Where is this documented?
<--- Score

125. How does the Leadership styles manager ensure against scope creep?
<--- Score

126. What Leadership styles services do you require?
<--- Score

127. Is the team adequately staffed with the desired cross-functionality? If not, what additional resources are available to the team?
<--- Score

128. Is data collected and displayed to better understand customer(s) critical needs and requirements.

<--- Score

129. Is Leadership styles required?
<--- Score

130. How can the value of Leadership styles be defined?
<--- Score

131. What happens if Leadership styles's scope changes?
<--- Score

132. What gets examined?
<--- Score

133. Do you have a Leadership styles success story or case study ready to tell and share?
<--- Score

134. How would you define the culture at your organization, how susceptible is it to Leadership styles changes?
<--- Score

135. If substitutes have been appointed, have they been briefed on the Leadership styles goals and received regular communications as to the progress to date?
<--- Score

136. What is in scope?
<--- Score

137. Is Leadership styles currently on schedule according to the plan?

<--- Score

138. What are (control) requirements for Leadership styles Information?
<--- Score

139. The political context: who holds power?
<--- Score

140. Is Leadership styles linked to key stakeholder goals and objectives?
<--- Score

141. Is the Leadership styles scope manageable?
<--- Score

Add up total points for this section:
_____ = Total points for this section

Divided by: _____ (number of statements answered) = _____
Average score for this section

Transfer your score to the Leadership styles Index at the beginning of the Self-Assessment.

CRITERION #3: MEASURE:

INTENT: Gather the correct data.
Measure the current performance and
evolution of the situation.

In my belief, the answer to this
question is clearly defined:

5 Strongly Agree

4 Agree

3 Neutral

2 Disagree

1 Strongly Disagree

1. Are you taking your company in the direction of better and revenue or cheaper and cost?
<--- Score

2. Is the solution cost-effective?
<--- Score

3. What are your key Leadership styles organizational performance measures, including key short and

longer-term financial measures?
<--- Score

4. How do your measurements capture actionable Leadership styles information for use in exceeding your customers expectations and securing your customers engagement?
<--- Score

5. Will Leadership styles have an impact on current business continuity, disaster recovery processes and/or infrastructure?
<--- Score

6. Where is the cost?
<--- Score

7. What could cause delays in the schedule?
<--- Score

8. Are there measurements based on task performance?
<--- Score

9. How do you verify the authenticity of the data and information used?
<--- Score

10. What is measured? Why?
<--- Score

11. What relevant entities could be measured?
<--- Score

12. How will your organization measure success?
<--- Score

13. Are the measurements objective?
<--- Score

14. What are the types and number of measures to use?
<--- Score

15. Who pays the cost?
<--- Score

16. Do the benefits outweigh the costs?
<--- Score

17. How can you measure Leadership styles in a systematic way?
<--- Score

18. What causes innovation to fail or succeed in your organization?
<--- Score

19. How do you measure variability?
<--- Score

20. Are actual costs in line with budgetec costs?
<--- Score

21. What are the estimated costs of proposed changes?
<--- Score

22. Do you have a flow diagram of what happens?
<--- Score

23. What measurements are possible, practicable and

meaningful?
<--- Score

24. How will measures be used to manage and adapt?
<--- Score

25. What do people want to verify?
<--- Score

26. How long to keep data and how to manage retention costs?
<--- Score

27. What is the root cause(s) of the problem?
<--- Score

28. Does a Leadership styles quantification method exist?
<--- Score

29. What drives O&M cost?
<--- Score

30. What are the costs and benefits?
<--- Score

31. What harm might be caused?
<--- Score

32. Does the Leadership styles task fit the client's priorities?
<--- Score

33. What is the Leadership styles business impact?
<--- Score

34. How do you verify and validate the Leadership styles data?
<--- Score

35. Are Leadership styles vulnerabilities categorized and prioritized?
<--- Score

36. What can be used to verify compliance?
<--- Score

37. Which measures and indicators matter?
<--- Score

38. How do you measure success?
<--- Score

39. What are your customers expectations and measures?
<--- Score

40. What is your Leadership styles quality cost segregation study?
<--- Score

41. What evidence is there and what is measured?
<--- Score

42. What causes mismanagement?
<--- Score

43. Are you able to realize any cost savings?
<--- Score

44. Did you tackle the cause or the symptom?
<--- Score

45. Are the Leadership styles benefits worth its costs?
<--- Score

46. How will success or failure be measured?
<--- Score

47. How can you measure the performance?
<--- Score

48. What are the Leadership styles key cost drivers?
<--- Score

49. Who is involved in verifying compliance?
<--- Score

50. Does management have the right priorities among projects?
<--- Score

51. How do you verify the Leadership styles requirements quality?
<--- Score

52. What could cause you to change course?
<--- Score

53. Which costs should be taken into account?
<--- Score

54. Are you aware of what could cause a problem?
<--- Score

55. How do you verify Leadership styles completeness and accuracy?
<--- Score

56. Have you made assumptions about the shape of the future, particularly its impact on your customers and competitors?
<--- Score

57. What is an unallowable cost?
<--- Score

58. What details are required of the Leadership styles cost structure?
<--- Score

59. What are the strategic priorities for this year?
<--- Score

60. What are the operational costs after Leadership styles deployment?
<--- Score

61. How do you verify performance?
<--- Score

62. Are indirect costs charged to the Leadership styles program?
<--- Score

63. What tests verify requirements?
<--- Score

64. What potential environmental factors impact the Leadership styles effort?
<--- Score

65. When should you bother with diagrams?
<--- Score

66. Are there competing Leadership styles priorities?
<--- Score

67. What are the current costs of the Leadership styles process?
<--- Score

68. How is the value delivered by Leadership styles being measured?
<--- Score

69. What would it cost to replace your technology?
<--- Score

70. What are the costs?
<--- Score

71. What is the total fixed cost?
<--- Score

72. What would be a real cause for concern?
<--- Score

73. What users will be impacted?
<--- Score

74. What do you measure and why?
<--- Score

75. Do you have any cost Leadership styles limitation requirements?
<--- Score

76. How do you quantify and qualify impacts?
<--- Score

77. What are you verifying?
<--- Score

78. What are your primary costs, revenues, assets?
<--- Score

79. Among the Leadership styles product and service cost to be estimated, which is considered hardest to estimate?
<--- Score

80. How can you reduce the costs of obtaining inputs?
<--- Score

81. What are the Leadership styles investment costs?
<--- Score

82. How are measurements made?
<--- Score

83. Do you verify that corrective actions were taken?
<--- Score

84. When a disaster occurs, who gets priority?
<--- Score

85. How are you verifying it?
<--- Score

86. Is there an opportunity to verify requirements?
<--- Score

87. How frequently do you track Leadership styles measures?
<--- Score

88. How do you verify your resources?
<--- Score

89. At what cost?
<--- Score

90. How do you aggregate measures across priorities?
<--- Score

91. What are the costs of delaying Leadership styles action?
<--- Score

92. What measurements are being captured?
<--- Score

93. How is performance measured?
<--- Score

94. How will costs be allocated?
<--- Score

95. How can a Leadership styles test verify your ideas or assumptions?
<--- Score

96. Are supply costs steady or fluctuating?
<--- Score

97. Why a Leadership styles focus?
<--- Score

98. How sensitive must the Leadership styles strategy be to cost?
<--- Score

99. Has a cost center been established?
<--- Score

100. When are costs are incurred?
<--- Score

101. The approach of traditional Leadership styles works for detail complexity but is focused on a systematic approach rather than an understanding of the nature of systems themselves, what approach will permit your organization to deal with the kind of unpredictable emergent behaviors that dynamic complexity can introduce?
<--- Score

102. How do you verify if Leadership styles is built right?
<--- Score

103. What does a Test Case verify?
<--- Score

104. Do you aggressively reward and promote the people who have the biggest impact on creating excellent Leadership styles services/products?
<--- Score

105. Where is it measured?
<--- Score

106. What are your operating costs?
<--- Score

107. How can you reduce costs?
<--- Score

108. What are the uncertainties surrounding estimates of impact?
<--- Score

109. Who should receive measurement reports?
<--- Score

110. How can you manage cost down?
<--- Score

111. How do you measure lifecycle phases?
<--- Score

112. What is the cost of rework?
<--- Score

113. Do you have an issue in getting priority?
<--- Score

114. Where can you go to verify the info?
<--- Score

115. How will you measure success?
<--- Score

116. What methods are feasible and acceptable to estimate the impact of reforms?
<--- Score

117. How to cause the change?
<--- Score

118. What does losing customers cost your organization?
<--- Score

119. Is it possible to estimate the impact of unanticipated complexity such as wrong or failed assumptions, feedback, etcetera on proposed reforms?
<--- Score

120. Do you effectively measure and reward individual and team performance?
<--- Score

121. What causes investor action?
<--- Score

122. What are allowable costs?
<--- Score

123. What are hidden Leadership styles quality costs?
<--- Score

124. What are the costs of reform?
<--- Score

125. How do you focus on what is right -not who is right?
<--- Score

126. What happens if cost savings do not materialize?
<--- Score

127. What causes extra work or rework?
<--- Score

128. What is the cause of any Leadership styles gaps?
<--- Score

129. How do you control the overall costs of your work processes?
<--- Score

130. What does verifying compliance entail?
<--- Score

131. How frequently do you verify your Leadership styles strategy?
<--- Score

Add up total points for this section:
_____ = Total points for this section

Divided by: _____ (number of statements answered) = _____
Average score for this section

Transfer your score to the Leadership styles Index at the beginning of the Self-Assessment.

CRITERION #4: ANALYZE:

INTENT: Analyze causes, assumptions and hypotheses.

In my belief, the answer to this question is clearly defined:

5 Strongly Agree

4 Agree

3 Neutral

2 Disagree

1 Strongly Disagree

1. Who gets your output?
<--- Score

2. Is pre-qualification of suppliers carried out?
<--- Score

3. What are the best opportunities for value improvement?
<--- Score

4. Do staff qualifications match your project?
<--- Score

5. Is there any way to speed up the process?
<--- Score

6. Did any additional data need to be collected?
<--- Score

7. What are your key performance measures or indicators and in-process measures for the control and improvement of your Leadership styles processes?
<--- Score

8. What Leadership styles data do you gather or use now?
<--- Score

9. An organizationally feasible system request is one that considers the mission, goals and objectives of the organization, key questions are: is the Leadership styles solution request practical and will it solve a problem or take advantage of an opportunity to achieve company goals?
<--- Score

10. How do you define collaboration and team output?
<--- Score

11. What data do you need to collect?
<--- Score

12. What information qualified as important?
<--- Score

13. Who is involved in the management review process?
<--- Score

14. Do you have the authority to produce the output?
<--- Score

15. What quality tools were used to get through the analyze phase?
<--- Score

16. What are your current levels and trends in key Leadership styles measures or indicators of product and process performance that are important to and directly serve your customers?
<--- Score

17. Have the problem and goal statements been updated to reflect the additional knowledge gained from the analyze phase?
<--- Score

18. What systems/processes must you excel at?
<--- Score

19. Has an output goal been set?
<--- Score

20. How do you measure the operational performance of your key work systems and processes, including productivity, cycle time, and other appropriate measures of process effectiveness, efficiency, and innovation?
<--- Score

21. Do several people in different organizational units

assist with the Leadership styles process?
<--- Score

22. What are the processes for audit reporting and management?
<--- Score

23. What Leadership styles data should be managed?
<--- Score

24. What were the crucial 'moments of truth' on the process map?
<--- Score

25. Do you understand your management processes today?
<--- Score

26. Do your employees have the opportunity to do what they do best everyday?
<--- Score

27. Do you, as a leader, bounce back quickly from setbacks?
<--- Score

28. What types of data do your Leadership styles indicators require?
<--- Score

29. Think about some of the processes you undertake within your organization, which do you own?
<--- Score

30. Are all staff in core Leadership styles subjects Highly Qualified?

<--- Score

31. Were any designed experiments used to generate additional insight into the data analysis?
<--- Score

32. What Leadership styles data should be collected?
<--- Score

33. What conclusions were drawn from the team's data collection and analysis? How did the team reach these conclusions?
<--- Score

34. Who will facilitate the team and process?
<--- Score

35. Which Leadership styles data should be retained?
<--- Score

36. What are your current levels and trends in key measures or indicators of Leadership styles product and process performance that are important to and directly serve your customers? How do these results compare with the performance of your competitors and other organizations with similar offerings?
<--- Score

37. When should a process be art not science?
<--- Score

38. Were Pareto charts (or similar) used to portray the 'heavy hitters' (or key sources of variation)?
<--- Score

39. What will drive Leadership styles change?

<--- Score

40. Who qualifies to gain access to data?
<--- Score

41. Is the gap/opportunity displayed and communicated in financial terms?
<--- Score

42. How do mission and objectives affect the Leadership styles processes of your organization?
<--- Score

43. Are you missing Leadership styles opportunities?
<--- Score

44. How difficult is it to qualify what Leadership styles ROI is?
<--- Score

45. What did the team gain from developing a sub-process map?
<--- Score

46. How will the data be checked for quality?
<--- Score

47. What successful thing are you doing today that may be blinding you to new growth opportunities?
<--- Score

48. What resources go in to get the desired output?
<--- Score

49. What Leadership styles data will be collected?
<--- Score

50. What are the Leadership styles design outputs?
<--- Score

51. How has the Leadership styles data been gathered?
<--- Score

52. How much data can be collected in the given timeframe?
<--- Score

53. Is the performance gap determined?
<--- Score

54. Who is involved with workflow mapping?
<--- Score

55. How does the organization define, manage, and improve its Leadership styles processes?
<--- Score

56. How will corresponding data be collected?
<--- Score

57. What controls do you have in place to protect data?
<--- Score

58. How are outputs preserved and protected?
<--- Score

59. How do you implement and manage your work processes to ensure that they meet design requirements?
<--- Score

60. Is the required Leadership styles data gathered?
<--- Score

61. How was the detailed process map generated, verified, and validated?
<--- Score

62. How is Leadership styles data gathered?
<--- Score

63. What training and qualifications will you need?
<--- Score

64. Was a cause-and-effect diagram used to explore the different types of causes (or sources of variation)?
<--- Score

65. Should you invest in industry-recognized qualifications?
<--- Score

66. Identify an operational issue in your organization, for example, could a particular task be done more quickly or more efficiently by Leadership styles?
<--- Score

67. Is the final output clearly identified?
<--- Score

68. How is data used for program management and improvement?
<--- Score

69. Can you add value to the current Leadership styles decision-making process (largely qualitative)

by incorporating uncertainty modeling (more quantitative)?
<--- Score

70. What qualifications are needed?
<--- Score

71. What process improvements will be needed?
<--- Score

72. Is the suppliers process defined and controlled?
<--- Score

73. Do your contracts/agreements contain data security obligations?
<--- Score

74. What are your Leadership styles processes?
<--- Score

75. A compounding model resolution with available relevant data can often provide insight towards a solution methodology; which Leadership styles models, tools and techniques are necessary?
<--- Score

76. What are evaluation criteria for the output?
<--- Score

77. How do you identify specific Leadership styles investment opportunities and emerging trends?
<--- Score

78. Have any additional benefits been identified that will result from closing all or most of the gaps?
<--- Score

79. How often will data be collected for measures?
<--- Score

80. What is the cost of poor quality as supported by the team's analysis?
<--- Score

81. Was a detailed process map created to amplify critical steps of the 'as is' stakeholder process?
<--- Score

82. What are the Leadership styles business drivers?
<--- Score

83. What methods do you use to gather Leadership styles data?
<--- Score

84. How do you ensure that the Leadership styles opportunity is realistic?
<--- Score

85. What Leadership styles metrics are outputs of the process?
<--- Score

86. Did any value-added analysis or 'lean thinking' take place to identify some of the gaps shown on the 'as is' process map?
<--- Score

87. What is your organizations process which leads to recognition of value generation?
<--- Score

88. What is the complexity of the output produced?
<--- Score

89. Is data and process analysis, root cause analysis and quantifying the gap/opportunity in place?
<--- Score

90. What is the Leadership styles Driver?
<--- Score

91. Is the Leadership styles process severely broken such that a re-design is necessary?
<--- Score

92. What is the output?
<--- Score

93. How will the Leadership styles data be captured?
<--- Score

94. What tools were used to narrow the list of possible causes?
<--- Score

95. Are gaps between current performance and the goal performance identified?
<--- Score

96. Where is Leadership styles data gathered?
<--- Score

97. How many input/output points does it require?
<--- Score

98. How is the Leadership styles Value Stream Mapping managed?

<--- Score

99. What are your best practices for minimizing Leadership styles project risk, while demonstrating incremental value and quick wins throughout the Leadership styles project lifecycle?
<--- Score

100. Do quality systems drive continuous improvement?
<--- Score

101. What internal processes need improvement?
<--- Score

102. What are the personnel training and qualifications required?
<--- Score

103. What does the data say about the performance of the stakeholder process?
<--- Score

104. Record-keeping requirements flow from the records needed as inputs, outputs, controls and for transformation of a Leadership styles process, are the records needed as inputs to the Leadership styles process available?
<--- Score

105. What were the financial benefits resulting from any 'ground fruit or low-hanging fruit' (quick fixes)?
<--- Score

106. What qualifications do Leadership styles leaders need?

<--- Score

107. How will the change process be managed?
<--- Score

108. What, related to, Leadership styles processes does your organization outsource?
<--- Score

109. What qualifies as competition?
<--- Score

110. Has data output been validated?
<--- Score

111. Have you defined which data is gathered how?
<--- Score

112. What qualifications and skills do you need?
<--- Score

113. Are Leadership styles changes recognized early enough to be approved through the regular process?
<--- Score

114. What are your outputs?
<--- Score

115. Where can you get qualified talent today?
<--- Score

116. What kind of crime could a potential new hire have committed that would not only not disqualify him/her from being hired by your organization, but would actually indicate that he/she might be a particularly good fit?

<--- Score

117. How can risk management be tied procedurally to process elements?
<--- Score

118. How is the way you as the leader think and process information affecting your organizational culture?
<--- Score

119. What other jobs or tasks affect the performance of the steps in the Leadership styles process?
<--- Score

120. Who owns what data?
<--- Score

121. What is the oversight process?
<--- Score

122. What other organizational variables, such as reward systems or communication systems, affect the performance of this Leadership styles process?
<--- Score

123. What is the Value Stream Mapping?
<--- Score

124. What do you need to qualify?
<--- Score

125. What tools were used to generate the list of possible causes?
<--- Score

126. Who will gather what data?
<--- Score

127. What are the revised rough estimates of the financial savings/opportunity for Leadership styles improvements?
<--- Score

128. Is there a strict change management process?
<--- Score

129. Do your leaders quickly bounce back from setbacks?
<--- Score

130. Were there any improvement opportunities identified from the process analysis?
<--- Score

131. How do your work systems and key work processes relate to and capitalize on your core competencies?
<--- Score

132. How is the data gathered?
<--- Score

Add up total points for this section:
_____ = Total points for this section

Divided by: _____ (number of statements answered) = _____
Average score for this section

Transfer your score to the Leadership styles Index at the beginning of the

Self-Assessment.

CRITERION #5: IMPROVE:

INTENT: Develop a practical solution. Innovate, establish and test the solution and to measure the results.

In my belief, the answer to this question is clearly defined:

5 Strongly Agree

4 Agree

3 Neutral

2 Disagree

1 Strongly Disagree

1. What is Leadership styles's impact on utilizing the best solution(s)?
<--- Score

2. Do you have the optimal project management team structure?
<--- Score

3. Is a contingency plan established?

<--- Score

4. How do you link measurement and risk?
<--- Score

5. What communications are necessary to support the implementation of the solution?
<--- Score

6. Who are the Leadership styles decision makers?
<--- Score

7. Do you need to do a usability evaluation?
<--- Score

8. Who controls key decisions that will be made?
<--- Score

9. Who do you report Leadership styles results to?
<--- Score

10. How will you know when its improved?
<--- Score

11. Is the Leadership styles documentation thorough?
<--- Score

12. Can you integrate quality management and risk management?
<--- Score

13. How will you know that you have improved?
<--- Score

14. Are risk triggers captured?
<--- Score

15. Where do you need Leadership styles improvement?
<--- Score

16. How can you improve Leadership styles?
<--- Score

17. Who makes the Leadership styles decisions in your organization?
<--- Score

18. Is the solution technically practical?
<--- Score

19. What tools were most useful during the improve phase?
<--- Score

20. What error proofing will be done to address some of the discrepancies observed in the 'as is' process?
<--- Score

21. What is the team's contingency plan for potential problems occurring in implementation?
<--- Score

22. What area needs the greatest improvement?
<--- Score

23. Risk events: what are the things that could go wrong?
<--- Score

24. What assumptions are made about the solution and approach?

<--- Score

25. How do you measure improved Leadership styles service perception, and satisfaction?
<--- Score

26. How do you go about comparing Leadership styles approaches/solutions?
<--- Score

27. How risky is your organization?
<--- Score

28. Are risk management tasks balanced centrally and locally?
<--- Score

29. Do you cover the five essential competencies: Communication, Collaboration, Innovation, Adaptability, and Leadership that improve an organizations ability to leverage the new Leadership styles in a volatile global economy?
<--- Score

30. Was a Leadership styles charter developed?
<--- Score

31. Do vendor agreements bring new compliance risk ?
<--- Score

32. How scalable is your Leadership styles solution?
<--- Score

33. Who manages Leadership styles risk?
<--- Score

34. What were the underlying assumptions on the cost-benefit analysis?
<--- Score

35. How do you measure progress and evaluate training effectiveness?
<--- Score

36. What practices helps your organization to develop its capacity to recognize patterns?
<--- Score

37. When you map the key players in your own work and the types/domains of relationships with them, which relationships do you find easy and which challenging, and why?
<--- Score

38. What resources are required for the improvement efforts?
<--- Score

39. How does your organization evaluate strategic Leadership styles success?
<--- Score

40. What needs improvement? Why?
<--- Score

41. If you could go back in time five years, what decision would you make differently? What is your best guess as to what decision you're making today you might regret five years from now?
<--- Score

42. Is the optimal solution selected based on testing and analysis?
<--- Score

43. How will you recognize and celebrate results?
<--- Score

44. What is the implementation plan?
<--- Score

45. For decision problems, how do you develop a decision statement?
<--- Score

46. Are you assessing Leadership styles and risk?
<--- Score

47. How will you know that a change is an improvement?
<--- Score

48. How do you keep improving Leadership styles?
<--- Score

49. How is continuous improvement applied to risk management?
<--- Score

50. Who will be using the results of the measurement activities?
<--- Score

51. Leadership styles risk decisions: whose call Is It?
<--- Score

52. Who will be responsible for documenting the

Leadership styles requirements in detail?
<--- Score

53. Who are the key stakeholders for the Leadership styles evaluation?
<--- Score

54. Does a good decision guarantee a good outcome?
<--- Score

55. Is the Leadership styles risk managed?
<--- Score

56. Is Leadership styles documentation maintained?
<--- Score

57. Are the most efficient solutions problem-specific?
<--- Score

58. How do you manage and improve your Leadership styles work systems to deliver customer value and achieve organizational success and sustainability?
<--- Score

59. What are the implications of the one critical Leadership styles decision 10 minutes, 10 months, and 10 years from now?
<--- Score

60. How do you mitigate Leadership styles risk?
<--- Score

61. What should a proof of concept or pilot accomplish?
<--- Score

62. Can the solution be designed and implemented within an acceptable time period?
<--- Score

63. Is there a cost/benefit analysis of optimal solution(s)?
<--- Score

64. How can you improve performance?
<--- Score

65. What does the 'should be' process map/design look like?
<--- Score

66. Who will be responsible for making the decisions to include or exclude requested changes once Leadership styles is underway?
<--- Score

67. Are decisions made in a timely manner?
<--- Score

68. What attendant changes will need to be made to ensure that the solution is successful?
<--- Score

69. Is there a small-scale pilot for proposed improvement(s)? What conclusions were drawn from the outcomes of a pilot?
<--- Score

70. What strategies for Leadership styles improvement are successful?
<--- Score

71. In the past few months, what is the smallest change you have made that has had the biggest positive result? What was it about that small change that produced the large return?
<--- Score

72. What is the magnitude of the improvements?
<--- Score

73. How are Leadership styles risks managed?
<--- Score

74. How do you define the solutions' scope?
<--- Score

75. Is risk periodically assessed?
<--- Score

76. Is pilot data collected and analyzed?
<--- Score

77. Is the scope clearly documented?
<--- Score

78. What tools were used to tap into the creativity and encourage 'outside the box' thinking?
<--- Score

79. Where do the Leadership styles decisions reside?
<--- Score

80. Are the risks fully understood, reasonable and manageable?
<--- Score

81. How does the team improve its work?

<--- Score

82. Is any Leadership styles documentation required?
<--- Score

83. Is supporting Leadership styles documentation required?
<--- Score

84. Who controls the risk?
<--- Score

85. What tools were used to evaluate the potential solutions?
<--- Score

86. Is there any other Leadership styles solution?
<--- Score

87. How can the phases of Leadership styles development be identified?
<--- Score

88. What are the expected Leadership styles results?
<--- Score

89. Explorations of the frontiers of Leadership styles will help you build influence, improve Leadership styles, optimize decision making, and sustain change, what is your approach?
<--- Score

90. Why improve in the first place?
<--- Score

91. What are the affordable Leadership styles risks?

<--- Score

92. How do you improve Leadership styles service perception, and satisfaction?
<--- Score

93. Which of the recognised risks out of all risks can be most likely transferred?
<--- Score

94. Are the key business and technology risks being managed?
<--- Score

95. What Leadership styles improvements can be made?
<--- Score

96. What were the criteria for evaluating a Leadership styles pilot?
<--- Score

97. What are your current levels and trends in key measures or indicators of workforce and leader development?
<--- Score

98. How is knowledge sharing about risk management improved?
<--- Score

99. Would you develop a Leadership styles Communication Strategy?
<--- Score

100. How will you measure the results?

<--- Score

101. Risk factors: what are the characteristics of Leadership styles that make it risky?
<--- Score

102. How do you improve your likelihood of success?
<--- Score

103. How do the Leadership styles results compare with the performance of your competitors and other organizations with similar offerings?
<--- Score

104. Who manages supplier risk management in your organization?
<--- Score

105. Is the implementation plan designed?
<--- Score

106. How do you improve productivity?
<--- Score

107. What current systems have to be understood and/or changed?
<--- Score

108. What is the risk?
<--- Score

109. Are procedures documented for managing Leadership styles risks?
<--- Score

110. What is Leadership styles risk?

<--- Score

111. Have you identified breakpoints and/or risk tolerances that will trigger broad consideration of a potential need for intervention or modification of strategy?
<--- Score

112. How do you deal with Leadership styles risk?
<--- Score

113. What to do with the results or outcomes of measurements?
<--- Score

114. Which Leadership styles solution is appropriate?
<--- Score

115. Is a solution implementation plan established, including schedule/work breakdown structure, resources, risk management plan, cost/budget, and control plan?
<--- Score

116. What are the Leadership styles security risks?
<--- Score

117. What alternative responses are available to manage risk?
<--- Score

118. What actually has to improve and by how much?
<--- Score

119. Will the controls trigger any other risks?
<--- Score

120. What is the Leadership styles's sustainability risk?
<--- Score

121. Is the measure of success for Leadership styles understandable to a variety of people?
<--- Score

122. How do you understand the leadership styles of the participant Principals?
<--- Score

123. Was a pilot designed for the proposed solution(s)?
<--- Score

124. For estimation problems, how do you develop an estimation statement?
<--- Score

125. Can you identify any significant risks or exposures to Leadership styles third- parties (vendors, service providers, alliance partners etc) that concern you?
<--- Score

126. Is there a high likelihood that any recommendations will achieve their intended results?
<--- Score

127. Who are the Leadership styles decision-makers?
<--- Score

128. How significant is the improvement in the eyes of the end user?
<--- Score

129. Who should make the Leadership styles decisions?
<--- Score

130. Is the Leadership styles solution sustainable?
<--- Score

131. What improvements have been achieved?
<--- Score

132. Are events managed to resolution?
<--- Score

133. What investment have you made to develop the leadership styles that support high levels of staff engagement?
<--- Score

134. What can you do to improve?
<--- Score

135. What lessons, if any, from a pilot were incorporated into the design of the full-scale solution?
<--- Score

136. Does the goal represent a desired result that can be measured?
<--- Score

137. Were any criteria developed to assist the team in testing and evaluating potential solutions?
<--- Score

138. How can you better manage risk?
<--- Score

139. What risks do you need to manage?
<--- Score

Add up total points for this section:
_____ = Total points for this section

Divided by: _____ (number of statements answered) = _____
Average score for this section

Transfer your score to the Leadership styles Index at the beginning of the Self-Assessment.

CRITERION #6: CONTROL:

INTENT: Implement the practical solution. Maintain the performance and correct possible complications.

In my belief, the answer to this question is clearly defined:

5 Strongly Agree

4 Agree

3 Neutral

2 Disagree

1 Strongly Disagree

1. You may have created your quality measures at a time when you lacked resources, technology wasn't up to the required standard, or low service levels were the industry norm. Have those circumstances changed?
<--- Score

2. Are there documented procedures?
<--- Score

3. Is there a Leadership styles Communication plan covering who needs to get what information when?
<--- Score

4. Are documented procedures clear and easy to follow for the operators?
<--- Score

5. Are pertinent alerts monitored, analyzed and distributed to appropriate personnel?
<--- Score

6. How will you measure your QA plan's effectiveness?
<--- Score

7. Will any special training be provided for results interpretation?
<--- Score

8. How will report readings be checked to effectively monitor performance?
<--- Score

9. What do you stand for--and what are you against?
<--- Score

10. Are you measuring, monitoring and predicting Leadership styles activities to optimize operations and profitability, and enhancing outcomes?
<--- Score

11. What should you measure to verify efficiency gains?
<--- Score

12. Will your goals reflect your program budget?
<--- Score

13. What are customers monitoring?
<--- Score

14. How will the process owner verify improvement in present and future sigma levels, process capabilities?
<--- Score

15. Are the Leadership styles standards challenging?
<--- Score

16. What quality tools were useful in the control phase?
<--- Score

17. How might the group capture best practices and lessons learned so as to leverage improvements?
<--- Score

18. Has the improved process and its steps been standardized?
<--- Score

19. How will Leadership styles decisions be made and monitored?
<--- Score

20. Is there a control plan in place for sustaining improvements (short and long-term)?
<--- Score

21. Is new knowledge gained imbedded in the response plan?
<--- Score

22. Is a response plan established and deployed?
<--- Score

23. Is there documentation that will support the successful operation of the improvement?
<--- Score

24. What can you control?
<--- Score

25. What Leadership styles standards are applicable?
<--- Score

26. How do you plan for the cost of succession?
<--- Score

27. How do you plan on providing proper recognition and disclosure of supporting companies?
<--- Score

28. How is change control managed?
<--- Score

29. Does a troubleshooting guide exist or is it needed?
<--- Score

30. Does Leadership styles appropriately measure and monitor risk?
<--- Score

31. What do your reports reflect?
<--- Score

32. How will the process owner and team be able to hold the gains?

<--- Score

33. How do you encourage people to take control and responsibility?
<--- Score

34. Is there a documented and implemented monitoring plan?
<--- Score

35. Can support from partners be adjusted?
<--- Score

36. Against what alternative is success being measured?
<--- Score

37. How will input, process, and output variables be checked to detect for sub-optimal conditions?
<--- Score

38. Does job training on the documented procedures need to be part of the process team's education and training?
<--- Score

39. Is there a standardized process?
<--- Score

40. Is there a transfer of ownership and knowledge to process owner and process team tasked with the responsibilities.
<--- Score

41. Are suggested corrective/restorative actions indicated on the response plan for known causes to

problems that might surface?
<--- Score

42. What are your results for key measures or indicators of the accomplishment of your Leadership styles strategy and action plans, including building and strengthening core competencies?
<--- Score

43. Do you monitor the effectiveness of your Leadership styles activities?
<--- Score

44. Has your organization learned new leadership styles or changed existing ones?
<--- Score

45. What is the standard for acceptable Leadership styles performance?
<--- Score

46. Is there a recommended audit plan for routine surveillance inspections of Leadership styles's gains?
<--- Score

47. What is the control/monitoring plan?
<--- Score

48. How widespread is its use?
<--- Score

49. Who has control over resources?
<--- Score

50. Do the Leadership styles decisions you make today help people and the planet tomorrow?

<--- Score

51. What is your theory of human motivation, and how does your compensation plan fit with that view?
<--- Score

52. How do you spread information?
<--- Score

53. What do you measure to verify effectiveness gains?
<--- Score

54. Is a response plan in place for when the input, process, or output measures indicate an 'out-of-control' condition?
<--- Score

55. Who is the Leadership styles process owner?
<--- Score

56. In the case of a Leadership styles project, the criteria for the audit derive from implementation objectives, an audit of a Leadership styles project involves assessing whether the recommendations outlined for implementation have been met, can you track that any Leadership styles project is implemented as planned, and is it working?
<--- Score

57. Are operating procedures consistent?
<--- Score

58. Who will be in control?
<--- Score

59. What should the next improvement project be that is related to Leadership styles?
<--- Score

60. Do you monitor the Leadership styles decisions made and fine tune them as they evolve?
<--- Score

61. What is the recommended frequency of auditing?
<--- Score

62. How do senior leaders actions reflect a commitment to the organizations Leadership styles values?
<--- Score

63. Are controls in place and consistently applied?
<--- Score

64. Who controls critical resources?
<--- Score

65. What are the performance and scale of the Leadership styles tools?
<--- Score

66. What is your plan to assess your security risks?
<--- Score

67. Can you adapt and adjust to changing Leadership styles situations?
<--- Score

68. Have new or revised work instructions resulted?
<--- Score

69. What are the critical parameters to watch?
<--- Score

70. How likely is the current Leadership styles plan to come in on schedule or on budget?
<--- Score

71. How do you establish and deploy modified action plans if circumstances require a shift in plans and rapid execution of new plans?
<--- Score

72. What is the best design framework for Leadership styles organization now that, in a post industrial-age if the top-down, command and control model is no longer relevant?
<--- Score

73. How do you select, collect, align, and integrate Leadership styles data and information for tracking daily operations and overall organizational performance, including progress relative to strategic objectives and action plans?
<--- Score

74. Are the planned controls in place?
<--- Score

75. Are the planned controls working?
<--- Score

76. How is Leadership styles project cost planned, managed, monitored?
<--- Score

77. What other systems, operations, processes, and

infrastructures (hiring practices, staffing, training, incentives/rewards, metrics/dashboards/scorecards, etc.) need updates, additions, changes, or deletions in order to facilitate knowledge transfer and improvements?
<--- Score

78. Who sets the Leadership styles standards?
<--- Score

79. Is the Leadership styles test/monitoring cost justified?
<--- Score

80. How will the day-to-day responsibilities for monitoring and continual improvement be transferred from the improvement team to the process owner?
<--- Score

81. Has the Leadership styles value of standards been quantified?
<--- Score

82. Does the Leadership styles performance meet the customer's requirements?
<--- Score

83. Where do ideas that reach policy makers and planners as proposals for Leadership styles strengthening and reform actually originate?
<--- Score

84. What key inputs and outputs are being measured on an ongoing basis?
<--- Score

85. How will new or emerging customer needs/requirements be checked/communicated to orient the process toward meeting the new specifications and continually reducing variation?
<--- Score

86. What are the known security controls?
<--- Score

87. Act/Adjust: What Do you Need to Do Differently?
<--- Score

88. Does the response plan contain a definite closed loop continual improvement scheme (e.g., plan-do-check-act)?
<--- Score

89. Is there an action plan in case of emergencies?
<--- Score

90. How do you monitor usage and cost?
<--- Score

91. Will existing staff require re-training, for example, to learn new business processes?
<--- Score

92. Is knowledge gained on process shared and institutionalized?
<--- Score

93. What are you attempting to measure/monitor?
<--- Score

94. How can you best use all of your knowledge

repositories to enhance learning and sharing?
<--- Score

95. What other areas of the group might benefit from the Leadership styles team's improvements, knowledge, and learning?
<--- Score

96. Is reporting being used or needed?
<--- Score

97. Do the viable solutions scale to future needs?
<--- Score

98. How do your controls stack up?
<--- Score

99. Are new process steps, standards, and documentation ingrained into normal operations?
<--- Score

100. How do controls support value?
<--- Score

101. Implementation Planning: is a pilot needed to test the changes before a full roll out occurs?
<--- Score

Add up total points for this section:
_____ = Total points for this section

Divided by: _____ (number of statements answered) = _____
Average score for this section

Transfer your score to the Leadership

styles Index at the beginning of the Self-Assessment.

CRITERION #7: SUSTAIN:

INTENT: Retain the benefits.

In my belief, the answer to this question is clearly defined:

5 Strongly Agree

4 Agree

3 Neutral

2 Disagree

1 Strongly Disagree

1. Do Leadership styles rules make a reasonable demand on a users capabilities?
<--- Score

2. If your customer were your grandmother, would you tell her to buy what you're selling?
<--- Score

3. If you find that you havent accomplished one of the goals for one of the steps of the Leadership styles strategy, what will you do to fix it?

<--- Score

4. Why are certain leadership styles more effective in certain situations?
<--- Score

5. How do you know if you are successful?
<--- Score

6. What is a feasible sequencing of reform initiatives over time?
<--- Score

7. Who is responsible for errors?
<--- Score

8. How do you think agile project management approach influences leadership?
<--- Score

9. What is effective Leadership styles?
<--- Score

10. How will you ensure you get what you expected?
<--- Score

11. How do you govern and fulfill your societal responsibilities?
<--- Score

12. Are you relevant? Will you be relevant five years from now? Ten?
<--- Score

13. How do you stay inspired?
<--- Score

14. How are you doing compared to your industry?
<--- Score

15. Do you think Leadership styles accomplishes the goals you expect it to accomplish?
<--- Score

16. Who is responsible for ensuring appropriate resources (time, people and money) are allocated to Leadership styles?
<--- Score

17. How will you know that the Leadership styles project has been successful?
<--- Score

18. What happens if you do not have enough funding?
<--- Score

19. What trophy do you want on your mantle?
<--- Score

20. What information is critical to your organization that your executives are ignoring?
<--- Score

21. What are you challenging?
<--- Score

22. What are the barriers to increased Leadership styles production?
<--- Score

23. What is the kind of project structure that would be

appropriate for your Leadership styles project, should it be formal and complex, or can it be less formal and relatively simple?
<--- Score

24. Is there any reason to believe the opposite of my current belief?
<--- Score

25. What are the essentials of internal Leadership styles management?
<--- Score

26. How likely is it that a customer would recommend your company to a friend or colleague?
<--- Score

27. How do you foster the skills, knowledge, talents, attributes, and characteristics you want to have?
<--- Score

28. How do you go about securing Leadership styles?
<--- Score

29. Is Leadership styles realistic, or are you setting yourself up for failure?
<--- Score

30. Is there any existing Leadership styles governance structure?
<--- Score

31. Has implementation been effective in reaching specified objectives so far?
<--- Score

32. Are assumptions made in Leadership styles stated explicitly?
<--- Score

33. What are the usability implications of Leadership styles actions?
<--- Score

34. What are leadership styles and habits that promote an ethical culture in a business?
<--- Score

35. What new services of functionality will be implemented next with Leadership styles ?
<--- Score

36. What happens at your organization when people fail?
<--- Score

37. How do you maintain Leadership styles's Integrity?
<--- Score

38. If you had to leave your organization for a year and the only communication you could have with employees/colleagues was a single paragraph, what would you write?
<--- Score

39. Who will provide the final approval of Leadership styles deliverables?
<--- Score

40. How does Leadership styles integrate with other stakeholder initiatives?
<--- Score

41. Can you maintain your growth without detracting from the factors that have contributed to your success?
<--- Score

42. How do you set Leadership styles stretch targets and how do you get people to not only participate in setting these stretch targets but also that they strive to achieve these?
<--- Score

43. What threat is Leadership styles addressing?
<--- Score

44. What one word do you want to own in the minds of your customers, employees, and partners?
<--- Score

45. How much contingency will be available in the budget?
<--- Score

46. What do we do when new problems arise?
<--- Score

47. Do you have the right people on the bus?
<--- Score

48. What happens when a new employee joins the organization?
<--- Score

49. Who do you want your customers to become?
<--- Score

50. What may be the consequences for the performance of an organization if all stakeholders are not consulted regarding Leadership styles?
<--- Score

51. What determines organization principals leadership styles?
<--- Score

52. Why will customers want to buy your organizations products/services?
<--- Score

53. If you do not follow, then how to lead?
<--- Score

54. What is the big Leadership styles idea?
<--- Score

55. What is the recommended frequency of auditing?
<--- Score

56. Can you break it down?
<--- Score

57. How do you determine the key elements that affect Leadership styles workforce satisfaction, how are these elements determined for different workforce groups and segments?
<--- Score

58. What is the overall business strategy?
<--- Score

59. How do you manage Leadership styles Knowledge Management (KM)?

<--- Score

60. What would have to be true for the option on the table to be the best possible choice?
<--- Score

61. What are the long-term Leadership styles goals?
<--- Score

62. What must you excel at?
<--- Score

63. Do you know who is a friend or a foe?
<--- Score

64. Ask yourself: how would you do this work if you only had one staff member to do it?
<--- Score

65. How do you assess the Leadership styles pitfalls that are inherent in implementing it?
<--- Score

66. What Leadership styles modifications can you make work for you?
<--- Score

67. In retrospect, of the projects that you pulled the plug on, what percent do you wish had been allowed to keep going, and what percent do you wish had ended earlier?
<--- Score

68. What knowledge, skills and characteristics mark a good Leadership styles project manager?
<--- Score

69. What should you stop doing?
<--- Score

70. Do you have an implicit bias for capital investments over people investments?
<--- Score

71. What is the overall talent health of your organization as a whole at senior levels, and for each organization reporting to a member of the Senior Leadership Team?
<--- Score

72. How do you keep the momentum going?
<--- Score

73. Do you say no to customers for no reason?
<--- Score

74. What is the estimated value of the project?
<--- Score

75. Think of your Leadership styles project, what are the main functions?
<--- Score

76. How is implementation research currently incorporated into each of your goals?
<--- Score

77. Do you see more potential in people than they do in themselves?
<--- Score

78. What are the management and leadership

styles?
<--- Score

79. Can the schedule be done in the given time?
<--- Score

80. Which functions and people interact with the supplier and or customer?
<--- Score

81. Who will determine interim and final deadlines?
<--- Score

82. Political -is anyone trying to undermine this project?
<--- Score

83. Are new benefits received and understood?
<--- Score

84. What are the business goals Leadership styles is aiming to achieve?
<--- Score

85. If your company went out of business tomorrow, would anyone who doesn't get a paycheck here care?
<--- Score

86. What are the top 3 things at the forefront of your Leadership styles agendas for the next 3 years?
<--- Score

87. How can you incorporate support to ensure safe and effective use of Leadership styles into the services that you provide?
<--- Score

88. What goals did you miss?
<--- Score

89. Is your basic point _____ or _____?
<--- Score

90. What have been your experiences in defining long range Leadership styles goals?
<--- Score

91. Are you / should you be revolutionary or evolutionary?
<--- Score

92. What trouble can you get into?
<--- Score

93. Do you have the right capabilities and capacities?
<--- Score

94. What are the leadership styles practiced by your organization principal?
<--- Score

95. What are the rules and assumptions your industry operates under? What if the opposite were true?
<--- Score

96. What are the key enablers to make this Leadership styles move?
<--- Score

97. Are all key stakeholders present at all Structured Walkthroughs?
<--- Score

98. If you were responsible for initiating and implementing major changes in your organization, what steps might you take to ensure acceptance of those changes?
<--- Score

99. Who uses your product in ways you never expected?
<--- Score

100. How do you deal with Leadership styles changes?
<--- Score

101. What stupid rule would you most like to kill?
<--- Score

102. Will there be any necessary staff changes (redundancies or new hires)?
<--- Score

103. What are internal and external Leadership styles relations?
<--- Score

104. Have benefits been optimized with all key stakeholders?
<--- Score

105. How can you negotiate Leadership styles successfully with a stubborn boss, an irate client, or a deceitful coworker?
<--- Score

106. How do you listen to customers to obtain actionable information?

<--- Score

107. How much does Leadership styles help?
<--- Score

108. What is your formula for success in Leadership styles ?
<--- Score

109. What are strategies for increasing support and reducing opposition?
<--- Score

110. What is the funding source for this project?
<--- Score

111. What did you miss in the interview for the worst hire you ever made?
<--- Score

112. How do leadership styles affect your organizations way of dealing with conflicts?
<--- Score

113. Do you have past Leadership styles successes?
<--- Score

114. In the past year, what have you done (or could you have done) to increase the accurate perception of your company/brand as ethical and honest?
<--- Score

115. What is it like to work for you?
<--- Score

116. Would you rather sell to knowledgeable and

informed customers or to uninformed customers?
<--- Score

117. What Leadership styles skills are most important?
<--- Score

118. Do you have enough freaky customers in your portfolio pushing you to the limit day in and day out?
<--- Score

119. What have you done to protect your business from competitive encroachment?
<--- Score

120. To whom do you add value?
<--- Score

121. If you got fired and a new hire took your place, what would she do different?
<--- Score

122. What are specific Leadership styles rules to follow?
<--- Score

123. Who else should you help?
<--- Score

124. If you had to rebuild your organization without any traditional competitive advantages (i.e., no killer technology, promising research, innovative product/service delivery model, etcetera), how would your people have to approach their work and collaborate together in order to create the necessary conditions for success?
<--- Score

125. Is there a work around that you can use?
<--- Score

126. How do you accomplish your long range Leadership styles goals?
<--- Score

127. Are you changing as fast as the world around you?
<--- Score

128. Do cultural values shape employee receptivity to leadership styles?
<--- Score

129. What are the challenges?
<--- Score

130. What business benefits will Leadership styles goals deliver if achieved?
<--- Score

131. Whom among your colleagues do you trust, and for what?
<--- Score

132. How do you transition from the baseline to the target?
<--- Score

133. Were lessons learned captured and communicated?
<--- Score

134. What projects are going on in the organization

today, and what resources are those projects using from the resource pools?
<--- Score

135. Have new benefits been realized?
<--- Score

136. Who do we want your customers to become?
<--- Score

137. How do you ensure that implementations of Leadership styles products are done in a way that ensures safety?
<--- Score

138. Do you think you know, or do you know you know ?
<--- Score

139. Why should you adopt a Leadership styles framework?
<--- Score

140. What are the success criteria that will indicate that Leadership styles objectives have been met and the benefits delivered?
<--- Score

141. What are the gaps in your knowledge and experience?
<--- Score

142. How do senior leaders deploy your organizations vision and values through your leadership system, to the workforce, to key suppliers and partners, and to customers and other stakeholders, as appropriate?

<--- Score

143. How will you motivate the stakeholders with the least vested interest?
<--- Score

144. How do customers see your organization?
<--- Score

145. If no one would ever find out about your accomplishments, how would you lead differently?
<--- Score

146. Is the impact that Leadership styles has shown?
<--- Score

147. What are the short and long-term Leadership styles goals?
<--- Score

148. When information truly is ubiquitous, when reach and connectivity are completely global, when computing resources are infinite, and when a whole new set of impossibilities are not only possible, but happening, what will that do to your business?
<--- Score

149. If you weren't already in this business, would you enter it today? And if not, what are you going to do about it?
<--- Score

150. Are there any activities that you can take off your to do list?
<--- Score

151. What role does communication play in the success or failure of a Leadership styles project?
<--- Score

152. How important is Leadership styles to the user organizations mission?
<--- Score

153. Why do and why don't your customers like your organization?
<--- Score

154. What is your question? Why?
<--- Score

155. Who will manage the integration of tools?
<--- Score

156. How do you foster innovation?
<--- Score

157. Is it economical; do you have the time and money?
<--- Score

158. Operational - will it work?
<--- Score

159. Who, on the executive team or the board, has spoken to a customer recently?
<--- Score

160. Are your responses positive or negative?
<--- Score

161. What is your BATNA (best alternative to a

negotiated agreement)?
<--- Score

162. Who will be responsible for deciding whether Leadership styles goes ahead or not after the initial investigations?
<--- Score

163. If there were zero limitations, what would you do differently?
<--- Score

164. Did your employees make progress today?
<--- Score

165. What potential megatrends could make your business model obsolete?
<--- Score

166. Is Leadership styles dependent on the successful delivery of a current project?
<--- Score

167. Are you paying enough attention to the partners your company depends on to succeed?
<--- Score

168. Why is Leadership styles important for you now?
<--- Score

169. Why servant leadership instead of other leadership styles?
<--- Score

170. What are the perceptions of employees towards organization directors leadership styles?

<--- Score

171. How do you create buy-in?
<--- Score

172. What are the potential basics of Leadership styles fraud?
<--- Score

173. Is a Leadership styles team work effort in place?
<--- Score

174. Leadership styles in technology acceptance: do followers practice what leaders preach?
<--- Score

175. How do different leadership styles link into different organizational emotions?
<--- Score

176. How can you become more high-tech but still be high touch?
<--- Score

177. Are you satisfied with your current role? If not, what is missing from it?
<--- Score

178. Which individuals, teams or departments will be involved in Leadership styles?
<--- Score

179. What is the craziest thing you can do?
<--- Score

180. What does your signature ensure?

<--- Score

181. Is your strategy driving your strategy? Or is the way in which you allocate resources driving your strategy?
<--- Score

182. What are current Leadership styles paradigms?
<--- Score

183. Is a Leadership styles breakthrough on the horizon?
<--- Score

184. What would you recommend your friend do if he/she were facing this dilemma?
<--- Score

185. Do you feel that more should be done in the Leadership styles area?
<--- Score

186. What management system can you use to leverage the Leadership styles experience, ideas, and concerns of the people closest to the work to be done?
<--- Score

187. Where can you break convention?
<--- Score

188. Are you making progress, and are you making progress as Leadership styles leaders?
<--- Score

189. Are you maintaining a past–present–future

perspective throughout the Leadership styles discussion?
<--- Score

190. How do you engage the workforce, in addition to satisfying them?
<--- Score

191. How do you keep records, of what?
<--- Score

192. Do you know what you are doing? And who do you call if you don't?
<--- Score

193. What is the source of the strategies for Leadership styles strengthening and reform?
<--- Score

194. Are you using a design thinking approach and integrating Innovation, Leadership styles Experience, and Brand Value?
<--- Score

195. Who is responsible for Leadership styles?
<--- Score

196. What is your competitive advantage?
<--- Score

197. What is something you believe that nearly no one agrees with you on?
<--- Score

198. How do you proactively clarify deliverables and Leadership styles quality expectations?

<--- Score

199. What could happen if you do not do it?
<--- Score

200. Are the assumptions believable and achievable?
<--- Score

201. Why not do Leadership styles?
<--- Score

202. At what moment would you think; Will I get fired?
<--- Score

203. Who are four people whose careers you have enhanced?
<--- Score

204. In a project to restructure Leadership styles outcomes, which stakeholders would you involve?
<--- Score

205. Which models, tools and techniques are necessary?
<--- Score

206. Whose voice (department, ethnic group, women, older workers, etc) might you have missed hearing from in your company, and how might you amplify this voice to create positive momentum for your business?
<--- Score

207. Who is on the team?
<--- Score

208. What are you trying to prove to yourself, and how might it be hijacking your life and business success?
<--- Score

209. How do you lead with Leadership styles in mind?
<--- Score

210. What are your personal philosophies regarding Leadership styles and how do they influence your work?
<--- Score

211. What skills and leadership styles contribute to effective directors?
<--- Score

212. What are your most important goals for the strategic Leadership styles objectives?
<--- Score

213. What is the purpose of Leadership styles in relation to the mission?
<--- Score

214. What counts that you are not counting?
<--- Score

215. Who do you think the world wants your organization to be?
<--- Score

216. Who is the main stakeholder, with ultimate responsibility for driving Leadership styles forward?
<--- Score

217. What you are going to do to affect the numbers?

<--- Score

218. How long will it take to change?
<--- Score

219. Which Leadership styles goals are the most important?
<--- Score

220. How do you cross-sell and up-sell your Leadership styles success?
<--- Score

221. Why is it important to have senior management support for a Leadership styles project?
<--- Score

222. Who have you, as a company, historically been when you've been at your best?
<--- Score

223. What was the last experiment you ran?
<--- Score

224. How do you make it meaningful in connecting Leadership styles with what users do day-to-day?
<--- Score

225. Why should people listen to you?
<--- Score

226. How do the leadership styles directly affect staff motivation?
<--- Score

227. What is the range of capabilities?

<--- Score

Add up total points for this sect on:
_____ = Total points for this section

Divided by: _____ (number of statements answered) = _____
Average score for this section

Transfer your score to the Leadership styles Index at the beginning of the Self-Assessment.

Leadership Styles and Managing Projects, Criteria for Project Managers:

1.0 Initiating Process Group: Leadership Styles

1. What must be done?

2. Do you understand all business (operational), technical, resource and vendor risks associated with the Leadership Styles project?

3. Do you understand the communication expectations for this Leadership Styles project?

4. Does the Leadership Styles project team have enough people to execute the Leadership Styles project plan?

5. Have you evaluated the teams performance and asked for feedback?

6. What were things that you did well, and could improve, and how?

7. Were sponsors and decision makers available when needed outside regularly scheduled meetings?

8. Where must it be done?

9. Who supports, improves, and oversees standardized processes related to the Leadership Styles projects program?

10. Are you certain deliverables are properly completed and meet quality standards?

11. What technical work to do in each phase?

12. Have requirements been tested, approved, and fulfill the Leadership Styles project scope?

13. How to control and approve each phase?

14. During which stage of Risk planning are modeling techniques used to determine overall effects of risks on Leadership Styles project objectives for high probability, high impact risks?

15. If action is called for, what form should it take?

16. During which stage of Risk planning are risks prioritized based on probability and impact?

17. Do you know the roles & responsibilities required for this Leadership Styles project?

18. The process to Manage Stakeholders is part of which process group?

19. What is the stake of others in your Leadership Styles project?

20. Were escalated issues resolved promptly?

1.1 Project Charter: Leadership Styles

21. Why have you chosen the aim you have set forth?

22. Does the Leadership Styles project need to consider any special capacity or capability issues?

23. Avoid costs, improve service, and/ or comply with a mandate?

24. Are you building in-house ?

25. When do you use a Leadership Styles project Charter?

26. How do you manage integration?

27. Why is it important?

28. What are you striving to accomplish (measurable goal(s))?

29. Where does all this information come from?

30. Who will take notes, document decisions?

31. How high should you set your goals?

32. Review the general mission What system will be affected by the improvement efforts?

33. What goes into your Leadership Styles project Charter?

34. What metrics could you look at?

35. Fit with other Products Compliments – Cannibalizes?

36. What are the deliverables?

37. Leadership Styles project objective statement: what must the Leadership Styles project do?

38. Customer benefits: what customer requirements does this Leadership Styles project address?

39. Assumptions and constraints: what assumptions were made in defining the Leadership Styles project?

40. Customer: who are you doing the Leadership Styles project for?

1.2 Stakeholder Register: Leadership Styles

41. Who wants to talk about Security?

42. How big is the gap?

43. What is the power of the stakeholder?

44. Who is managing stakeholder engagement?

45. How much influence do they have on the Leadership Styles project?

46. What are the major Leadership Styles project milestones requiring communications or providing communications opportunities?

47. How should employers make voices heard?

48. What opportunities exist to provide communications?

49. Who are the stakeholders?

50. Is your organization ready for change?

51. What & Why?

52. How will reports be created?

1.3 Stakeholder Analysis Matrix: Leadership Styles

53. Why involve the stakeholder?

54. Legislative effects?

55. Who has the power to influence the outcomes of the work?

56. Processes, systems, it, communications?

57. How can you counter negative efforts?

58. What do you need to appraise?

59. What makes a person a stakeholder?

60. Organizational Applicability?

61. New USPs?

62. Which conditions out of the control of the management are crucial for the achievement of the outputs?

63. Supporters; who are the supporters?

64. Are they likely to influence the success or failure of your Leadership Styles project?

65. How are the threatened Leadership Styles project targets being used?

66. Which conditions out of the control cf the management are crucial for the sustainability of its effects?

67. What should thwe organizations stakeholders avoid?

68. Tactics: eg, surprise, major contracts?

69. Which conditions out of the control of the management are crucial to contribute for the achievement of the development objective?

70. Partnerships, agencies, distribution?

71. Who is most dependent on the resources at stake?

72. What are the mechanisms of public and social accountability, and how can they be made better?

2.0 Planning Process Group: Leadership Styles

73. Is the pace of implementing the products of the program ensuring the completeness of the results of the Leadership Styles project?

74. When developing the estimates for Leadership Styles project phases, you choose to add the individual estimates for the activities that comprise each phase. What type of estimation method are you using?

75. Mitigate. what will you do to minimize the impact should a risk event occur?

76. Leadership Styles project assessment; why did you do this Leadership Styles project?

77. Is the identification of the problems, inequalities and gaps, with respective causes, clear in the Leadership Styles project?

78. What is a Software Development Life Cycle (SDLC)?

79. How can you make your needs known?

80. In what way has the Leadership Styles project come up with innovative measures for problem-solving?

81. How are it Leadership Styles projects different?

82. Is the duration of the program sufficient to ensure a cycle that will Leadership Styles project the sustainability of the interventions?

83. First of all, should any action be taken?

84. To what extent are the visions and actions of the partners consistent or divergent with regard to the program?

85. On which process should team members spend the most time?

86. How will it affect you?

87. Product breakdown structure (pbs): what is the Leadership Styles project result or product, and how should it look like, what are its parts?

88. To what extent have the target population and participants made the activities own, taking an active role in it?

89. How can you tell when you are done?

90. How does activity resource estimation affect activity duration estimation?

91. What will you do to minimize the impact should a risk event occur?

92. What do you need to do?

2.1 Project Management Plan: Leadership Styles

93. Who is the Leadership Styles project Manager?

94. Is there an incremental analysis/cost effectiveness analysis of proposed mitigation features based on an approved method and using an accepted model?

95. How well are you able to manage your risk?

96. Are cost risk analysis methods applied to develop contingencies for the estimated total Leadership Styles project costs?

97. If the Leadership Styles project management plan is a comprehensive document that guides you in Leadership Styles project execution and control, then what should it NOT contain?

98. Is the appropriate plan selected based on your organizations objectives and evaluation criteria expressed in Principles and Guidelines policies?

99. What are the constraints?

100. Is the budget realistic?

101. Are there any client staffing expectations?

102. Are alternatives safe, functional, constructible, economical, reasonable and sustainable?

103. If the Leadership Styles project is complex or scope is specialized, do you have appropriate and/or qualified staff available to perform the tasks?

104. Is mitigation authorized or recommended?

105. Why Change?

106. Development trends and opportunities. What if the positive direction and vision of your organization causes expected trends to change?

107. What happened during the process that you found interesting?

108. When is the Leadership Styles project management plan created?

109. How do you manage time?

2.2 Scope Management Plan: Leadership Styles

110. What if you do not have more detailed information on the report?

111. Are cause and effect determined for risks when they occur?

112. What happens to rejected deliverables?

113. What threats might prevent you from getting there?

114. Are the quality tools and methods identified in the Quality Plan appropriate to the Leadership Styles project?

115. Are there checklists created to demine if all quality processes are followed?

116. Do Leadership Styles project teams & team members report on status / activities / progress?

117. What weaknesses do you have?

118. Pop quiz – what changed on Leadership Styles project scope statement input?

119. Describe the process for rejecting the Leadership Styles project deliverables. What happens to rejected deliverables?

120. Are stakeholders aware and supportive of the principles and practices of modern software estimation?

121. Have external dependencies been captured in the schedule?

122. Are changes in deliverable commitments agreed to by all affected groups & individuals?

123. What happens if scope changes?

124. Would the Leadership Styles project cost sharing involve reimbursement to the sponsor?

125. Has process improvement efforts been completed before requirements efforts begin?

126. Will the Leadership Styles project deliverables become accepted in writing?

127. What are the acceptance criteria (process and criteria to be met for key stakeholder acceptance) and who is authorized to sign off?

128. Does a documented Leadership Styles project organizational policy & plan (i.e. governance model) exist?

129. Are milestone deliverables effectively tracked and compared to Leadership Styles project plan?

2.3 Requirements Management Plan: Leadership Styles

130. Why manage requirements?

131. Do you have price sheets and a methodology for determining the total proposal cost?

132. What cost metrics will be used?

133. Have stakeholders been instructed in the Change Control process?

134. How knowledgeable is the team in the proposed application area?

135. Does the Leadership Styles project have a Change Control process?

136. Will you perform a Requirements Risk assessment and develop a plan to deal with risks?

137. Did you get proper approvals?

138. Who came up with this requirement?

139. What went wrong?

140. Should you include sub-activities?

141. How will the requirements become prioritized?

142. Do you understand the role that each

stakeholder will play in the requirements process?

143. What is a problem?

144. Do you expect stakeholders to be ccoperative?

145. Has the requirements team been instructed in the Change Control process?

146. The wbs is developed as part of a joint planning session. and how do you know that youhave done this right?

147. Is there formal agreement on who has authority to request a change in requirements?

148. When and how will a requirements baseline be established in this Leadership Styles project?

149. What is the earliest finish date for this Leadership Styles project if it is scheduled to start on ...?

2.4 Requirements Documentation: Leadership Styles

150. What is the risk associated with cost and schedule?

151. What facilities must be supported by the system?

152. If applicable; are there issues linked with the fact that this is an offshore Leadership Styles project?

153. Are there any requirements conflicts?

154. Can the requirements be checked?

155. How do you get the user to tell you what they want?

156. Do technical resources exist?

157. Does the system provide the functions which best support the customers needs?

158. Is the origin of the requirement clearly stated?

159. What marketing channels do you want to use: e-mail, letter or sms?

160. Where are business rules being captured?

161. Validity. does the system provide the functions which best support the customers needs?

162. Is the requirement properly understood?

163. How does the proposed Leadership Styles project contribute to the overall objectives of your organization?

164. Consistency. are there any requirements conflicts?

165. Who is interacting with the system?

166. Has requirements gathering uncovered information that would necessitate changes?

167. What is a show stopper in the requirements?

168. Are all functions required by the customer included?

169. What will be the integration problems?

2.5 Requirements Traceability Matrix: Leadership Styles

170. How will it affect the stakeholders personally in career?

171. How do you manage scope?

172. What percentage of Leadership Styles projects are producing traceability matrices between requirements and other work products?

173. How small is small enough?

174. Is there a requirements traceability process in place?

175. Will you use a Requirements Traceability Matrix?

176. Why use a WBS?

177. What are the chronologies, contingencies, consequences, criteria?

178. What is the WBS?

179. Do you have a clear understanding of all subcontracts in place?

180. Describe the process for approving requirements so they can be added to the traceability matrix and Leadership Styles project work can be performed. Will the Leadership Styles project requirements become

approved in writing?

181. Why do you manage scope?

2.6 Project Scope Statement: Leadership Styles

182. Have the configuration management functions been assigned?

183. What is change?

184. Were potential customers involved early in the planning process?

185. How often will scope changes be reviewed?

186. Are there issues that could affect the existing requirements for the result, service, or product if the scope changes?

187. How will you verify the accuracy of the work of the Leadership Styles project, and what constitutes acceptance of the deliverables?

188. Do you anticipate new stakeholders joining the Leadership Styles project over time?

189. How often do you estimate that the scope might change, and why?

190. Has a method and process for requirement tracking been developed?

191. Change management vs. change leadership - what is the difference?

192. Are there specific processes you will use to evaluate and approve/reject changes?

193. Will all tasks resulting from issues be entered into the Leadership Styles project Plan and tracked through the plan?

194. Were key Leadership Styles project stakeholders brought into the Leadership Styles project Plan?

195. What is the most common tool for helping define the detail?

196. Will tasks be marked complete only after QA has been successfully completed?

197. Is an issue management process documented and filed?

198. Have you been able to easily identify success criteria and create objective measurements for each of the Leadership Styles project scopes goal statements?

199. Are the meetings set up to have assigned note takers that will add action/issues to the issue list?

200. Is there a Change Management Board?

2.7 Assumption and Constraint Log: Leadership Styles

201. What other teams / processes would be impacted by changes to the current process, and how?

202. If it is out of compliance, should the process be amended or should the Plan be amended?

203. How relevant is this attribute to this Leadership Styles project or audit?

204. How can constraints be violated?

205. Is this model reasonable?

206. Are you meeting your customers expectations consistently?

207. Does the plan conform to standards?

208. Are there processes defining how software will be developed including development methods, overall timeline for development, software product standards, and traceability?

209. Are there processes in place to ensure internal consistency between the source code components?

210. Are requirements management tracking tools and procedures in place?

211. After observing execution of process, is it in

compliance with the documented Plan?

212. Is there adequate stakeholder participation for the vetting of requirements definition, changes and management?

213. Does the document/deliverable meet all requirements (for example, statement of work) specific to this deliverable?

214. Was the document/deliverable developed per the appropriate or required standards (for example, Institute of Electrical and Electronics Engineers standards)?

215. Is there documentation of system capability requirements, data requirements, environment requirements, security requirements, and computer and hardware requirements?

216. Are there nonconformance issues?

217. Have all necessary approvals been obtained?

218. How can you prevent/fix violations?

219. What to do at recovery?

220. What do you audit?

2.8 Work Breakdown Structure: Leadership Styles

221. Is the work breakdown structure (wbs) defined and is the scope of the Leadership Styles project clear with assigned deliverable owners?

222. What is the probability that the Leadership Styles project duration will exceed xx weeks?

223. Who has to do it?

224. How many levels?

225. When do you stop?

226. Can you make it?

227. Do you need another level?

228. What has to be done?

229. Why would you develop a Work Breakdown Structure?

230. When would you develop a Work Breakdown Structure?

231. Where does it take place?

232. How far down?

233. When does it have to be done?

234. Is it still viable?

235. How big is a work-package?

236. What is the probability of completing the Leadership Styles project in less that xx days?

237. How much detail?

2.9 WBS Dictionary: Leadership Styles

238. Are overhead cost budgets (or Leadership Styles projections) established on a facility-wide basis at least annually for the life of the contract?

239. Authorization to proceed with all authorized work?

240. Are estimates of costs at completion generated in a rational, consistent manner?

241. Is all budget available as management reserve identified and excluded from the performance measurement baseline?

242. Performance to date and material commitment?

243. Where learning is used in developing underlying budgets is there a direct relationship between anticipated learning and time phased budgets?

244. Is future work which cannot be planned in detail subdivided to the extent practicable for budgeting and scheduling purposes?

245. Are the contractors estimates of costs at completion reconcilable with cost data reported to us?

246. Are material costs reported within the same period as that in which BCWP is earned for that material?

247. Should you have a test for each code module?

248. Changes in the nature of the overhead requirements?

249. What are you counting on?

250. Are overhead cost budgets established for each organization which has authority to incur overhead costs?

251. Can the contractor substantiate work package and planning package budgets?

252. What should you drop in order to add something new?

253. Appropriate work authorization documents which subdivide the contractual effort and responsibilities, within functional organizations?

254. Are management actions taken to reduce indirect costs when there are significant adverse variances?

255. Is the work done on a work package level as described in the WBS dictionary?

2.10 Schedule Management Plan: Leadership Styles

256. How does the proposed individual meet each requirement?

257. Is a process for scheduling and reporting defined, including forms and formats?

258. Are meeting minutes captured and sent out after the meeting?

259. Has the Leadership Styles project scope been baselined?

260. Do all stakeholders know how to access this repository and where to find the Leadership Styles project documentation?

261. What tools and techniques will be used to estimate activity resources?

262. Is there an issues management plan in place?

263. Have all documents been archived in a Leadership Styles project repository for each release?

264. What does a valid Schedule look like?

265. Is current scope of the Leadership Styles project substantially different than that originally defined?

266. Are all activities logically sequenced?

267. Must the Leadership Styles project be complete by a specified date?

268. Is the steering committee active in Leadership Styles project oversight?

269. Was your organizations estimating methodology being used and followed?

270. Perform reality checks on schedules – are all tasks included?

271. Goal: is the schedule feasible and at what cost?

272. Are Leadership Styles project contact logs kept up to date?

273. Have all involved Leadership Styles project stakeholders and work groups committed to the Leadership Styles project?

274. Are the Leadership Styles project plans updated on a frequent basis?

2.11 Activity List: Leadership Styles

275. How can the Leadership Styles project be displayed graphically to better visualize the activities?

276. Is there anything planned that does not need to be here?

277. How will it be performed?

278. For other activities, how much delay can be tolerated?

279. Is infrastructure setup part of your Leadership Styles project?

280. Can you determine the activity that must finish, before this activity can start?

281. How do you determine the late start (LS) for each activity?

282. When do the individual activities need to start and finish?

283. What went right?

284. What is your organizations history in doing similar activities?

285. What will be performed?

286. Who will perform the work?

287. What went well?

288. How should ongoing costs be monitored to try to keep the Leadership Styles project within budget?

289. Are the required resources available or need to be acquired?

290. What is the probability the Leadership Styles project can be completed in xx weeks?

291. When will the work be performed?

292. In what sequence?

293. What are the critical bottleneck activities?

2.12 Activity Attributes: Leadership Styles

294. How difficult will it be to complete specific activities on this Leadership Styles project?

295. What is missing?

296. Do you feel very comfortable with your prediction?

297. Resources to accomplish the work?

298. Has management defined a definite timeframe for the turnaround or Leadership Styles project window?

299. Time for overtime?

300. Would you consider either of corresponding activities an outlier?

301. How else could the items be grouped?

302. Resource is assigned to?

303. Activity: what is In the Bag?

304. Have constraints been applied to the start and finish milestones for the phases?

305. Where else does it apply?

306. Activity: fair or not fair?

307. How much activity detail is required?

308. Why?

309. Is there a trend during the year?

310. Can more resources be added?

2.13 Milestone List: Leadership Styles

311. Vital contracts and partners?

312. Loss of key staff?

313. Continuity, supply chain robustness?

314. Describe the industry you are in and the market growth opportunities. What is the market for your technology, product or service?

315. Global influences?

316. Do you foresee any technical risks or developmental challenges?

317. What are your competitors vulnerabilities?

318. Environmental effects?

319. Competitive advantages?

320. How late can the activity start?

321. Reliability of data, plan predictability?

322. What specific improvements did you make to the Leadership Styles project proposal since the previous time?

323. Obstacles faced?

324. Gaps in capabilities?

325. Describe the concept of the technology, product or service that will be or has been developed. How will it be used?

326. What is the market for your technology, product or service?

327. Which path is the critical path?

2.14 Network Diagram: Leadership Styles

328. Will crashing x weeks return more in benefits than it costs?

329. What is the completion time?

330. What activities must occur simultaneously with this activity?

331. What activity must be completed immediately before this activity can start?

332. What controls the start and finish of a job?

333. Why must you schedule milestones, such as reviews, throughout the Leadership Styles project?

334. Are the required resources available?

335. If a current contract exists, can you provide the vendor name, contract start, and contract expiration date?

336. Are the gantt chart and/or network diagram updated periodically and used to assess the overall Leadership Styles project timetable?

337. What is the probability of completing the Leadership Styles project in less that xx days?

338. What are the tools?

339. What to do and When?

340. Where do you schedule uncertainty time?

341. Planning: who, how long, what to do?

342. Where do schedules come from?

343. How difficult will it be to do specific activities on this Leadership Styles project?

344. What activities must follow this activity?

345. What job or jobs follow it?

346. What can be done concurrently?

2.15 Activity Resource Requirements: Leadership Styles

347. Why do you do that?

348. How do you handle petty cash?

349. What is the Work Plan Standard?

350. How many signatures do you require on a check and does this match what is in your policy and procedures?

351. Anything else?

352. When does monitoring begin?

353. What are constraints that you might find during the Human Resource Planning process?

354. Which logical relationship does the PDM use most often?

355. Other support in specific areas?

356. Do you use tools like decomposition and rolling-wave planning to produce the activity list and other outputs?

357. Are there unresolved issues that need to be addressed?

2.16 Resource Breakdown Structure: Leadership Styles

358. Who will use the system?

359. Why is this important?

360. Who delivers the information?

361. Is predictive resource analysis being done?

362. Why time management?

363. When do they need the information?

364. Who is allowed to perform which functions?

365. What defines a successful Leadership Styles project?

366. What is Leadership Styles project communication management?

367. Changes based on input from stakeholders?

368. Which resources should be in the resource pool?

369. What is each stakeholders desired outcome for the Leadership Styles project?

370. Which resource planning tool provides information on resource responsibility and accountability?

371. Why do you do it?

372. How difficult will it be to do specific activities on this Leadership Styles project?

373. Who is allowed to see what data about which resources?

2.17 Activity Duration Estimates: Leadership Styles

374. How do theories relate to Leadership Styles project management?

375. Describe Leadership Styles project integration management in your own words. How does Leadership Styles project integration management relate to the Leadership Styles project life cycle, stakeholders, and the other Leadership Styles project management knowledge areas?

376. What is the BEST thing to do?

377. Are expert judgment and historical information utilized to estimate activity duration?

378. Which suggestions do you find most useful?

379. Research recruiting and retention strategies at three different companies. What distinguishes one organization from another in this area?

380. Why is activity definition the first process involved in Leadership Styles project time management?

381. How is the Leadership Styles project doing?

382. Are updates on work results collected and used as inputs to the performance reporting process?

383. How does a Leadership Styles project life cycle differ from a product life cycle?

384. What type of contract was used and why?

385. What is earned value?

386. What are the main parts of a scope statement?

387. Does a process exist to identify which qualified resources may be attainable?

388. How do you enter durations, link tasks, and view critical path information?

389. Under corresponding circumstances what would be the best thing to do?

390. Are actual Leadership Styles project results compared with planned or expected results to determine the variance?

391. Who will provide inputs for it?

392. What is the critical path for this Leadership Styles project and how long is it?

2.18 Duration Estimating Worksheet: Leadership Styles

393. Why estimate costs?

394. Is this operation cost effective?

395. Will the Leadership Styles project collaborate with the local community and leverage resources?

396. How can the Leadership Styles project be displayed graphically to better visualize the activities?

397. What info is needed?

398. Can the Leadership Styles project be constructed as planned?

399. What is the total time required to complete the Leadership Styles project if no delays occur?

400. When does your organization expect to be able to complete it?

401. Why estimate time and cost?

402. Done before proceeding with this activity or what can be done concurrently?

403. What utility impacts are there?

404. What is next?

405. What is your role?

406. Is a construction detail attached (to aid in explanation)?

407. What work will be included in the Leadership Styles project?

2.19 Project Schedule: Leadership Styles

408. Your best shot for providing estimations how complex/how much work does the activity require?

409. Is there a Schedule Management Plan that establishes the criteria and activities for developing, monitoring and controlling the Leadership Styles project schedule?

410. How do you know that you have done this right?

411. Are activities connected because logic dictates the order in which others occur?

412. What is Leadership Styles project management?

413. What is the most mis-scheduled part of process?

414. How effectively were issues able to be resolved without impacting the Leadership Styles project Schedule or Budget?

415. Did the final product meet or exceed user expectations?

416. Why do you think schedule issues often cause the most conflicts on Leadership Styles projects?

417. Meet requirements?

418. How can you address that situation?

419. Activity charts and bar charts are graphical representations of a Leadership Styles project schedule ...how do they differ?

420. Is the structure for tracking the Leadership Styles project schedule well defined and assigned to a specific individual?

421. If you can not fix it, how do you do it differently?

422. Is infrastructure setup part of your Leadership Styles project?

423. It allows the Leadership Styles project to be delivered on schedule. How Do you Use Schedules?

424. How can you fix it?

2.20 Cost Management Plan: Leadership Styles

425. Is a pmo (Leadership Styles project management office) in place and provide oversight to the Leadership Styles project?

426. Is the steering committee active in Leadership Styles project oversight?

427. Are meeting objectives identified for each meeting?

428. Are tasks tracked by hours?

429. Leadership Styles project definition & scope?

430. Are risk triggers captured?

431. Responsibilities – what is the split of responsibilities between the owner and contractors?

432. Is your organization certified as a supplier, wholesaler and/or regular dealer?

433. Are all vendor contracts closed out?

434. Cost / benefit analysis?

435. Personnel with expertise?

436. Quality assurance overheads?

437. Is quality monitored from the perspective of the customers needs and expectations?

438. Does a documented Leadership Styles project organizational policy & plan (i.e. governance model) exist?

439. Are change requests logged and managed?

440. Cost variances – how will cost variances be identified and corrected?

441. Has a sponsor been identified?

442. Alignment to strategic goals & objectives?

443. Are the Leadership Styles project team members located locally to the users/stakeholders?

444. Does the schedule include Leadership Styles project management time and change request analysis time?

2.21 Activity Cost Estimates: Leadership Styles

445. Who determines the quality and expertise of contractors?

446. How difficult will it be to do specific tasks on the Leadership Styles project?

447. What defines a successful Leadership Styles project?

448. What do you want to know about the stay to know if costs were inappropriately high or low?

449. How do you change activities?

450. Can you change your activities?

451. Estimated cost?

452. Will you need to provide essential services information about activities?

453. One way to define activities is to consider how organization employees describe jobs to families and friends. You basically want to know, What do you do?

454. The impact and what actions were taken?

455. What communication items need improvement?

456. What areas were overlooked on this Leadership

Styles project?

457. Specific - is the objective clear in terms of what, how, when, and where the situation will be changed?

458. How do you do activity recasts?

459. Performance bond should always provide what part of the contract value?

460. In which phase of the acquisition process cycle does source qualifications reside?

461. Were you satisfied with the work?

462. Who determines when the contractor is paid?

463. Does the activity rely on a common set of tools to carry it out?

464. When do you enter into PPM?

2.22 Cost Estimating Worksheet: Leadership Styles

465. Ask: are others positioned to know, are others credible, and will others cooperate?

466. What additional Leadership Styles project(s) could be initiated as a result of this Leadership Styles project?

467. Does the Leadership Styles project provide innovative ways for stakeholders to overcome obstacles or deliver better outcomes?

468. What will others want?

469. Who is best positioned to know and assist in identifying corresponding factors?

470. Is the Leadership Styles project responsive to community need?

471. How will the results be shared and to whom?

472. Is it feasible to establish a control group arrangement?

473. What is the estimated labor cost today based upon this information?

474. What costs are to be estimated?

475. Value pocket identification & quantification what

are value pockets?

476. What happens to any remaining funds not used?

477. Can a trend be established from historical performance data on the selected measure and are the criteria for using trend analysis or forecasting methods met?

478. Will the Leadership Styles project collaborate with the local community and leverage resources?

479. What can be included?

480. What is the purpose of estimating?

481. Identify the timeframe necessary to monitor progress and collect data to determine how the selected measure has changed?

2.23 Cost Baseline: Leadership Styles

482. Is request in line with priorities?

483. Have the actual milestone completion dates been compared to the approved schedule?

484. Verify business objectives. Are others appropriate, and well-articulated?

485. Definition of done can be traced back to the definitions of what are you providing to the customer in terms of deliverables?

486. Does a process exist for establishing a cost baseline to measure Leadership Styles project performance?

487. Pcs for your new business. what would the life cycle costs be?

488. What can go wrong?

489. At which frequency ?

490. If you sold 10x widgets on a day, what would the affect on profits be?

491. How concrete were original objectives?

492. What strengths do you have?

493. How accurate do cost estimates need to be?

494. Why do you manage cost?

495. Who will use corresponding metrics ?

496. How difficult will it be to do specific tasks on the Leadership Styles project?

497. How fast?

498. What deliverables come first?

499. When should cost estimates be developed?

500. What is your organizations history in doing similar tasks?

2.24 Quality Management Plan: Leadership Styles

501. How do you decide who is responsible for signing the data reports?

502. What would you gain if you spent time working to improve this process?

503. Does the system design reflect the requirements?

504. Does the program conduct field testing?

505. What are the established criteria that sampling / testing data are compared against?

506. How do you decide what information to record?

507. What methods are used?

508. Have adequate resources been provided by management to ensure Leadership Styles project success?

509. What are your organizations current levels and trends for the already stated measures related to financial and marketplace performance?

510. What are your organizations current levels and trends for the already stated measures related to employee wellbeing, satisfaction, and development?

511. Are formal code reviews conducted?

512. Is the steering committee active in Leadership Styles project oversight?

513. You know what your customers expectations are regarding this process?

514. What data do you gather/use/compile?

515. What type of in-house testing do you conduct?

516. Have all involved stakeholders and work groups committed to the Leadership Styles project?

517. How are records kept in the office?

518. Has a Leadership Styles project Communications Plan been developed?

519. How will you know that a change is actually an improvement?

520. Do you periodically review your data quality system to see that it is up to date and appropriate?

2.25 Quality Metrics: Leadership Styles

521. Is material complete (and does it meet the standards)?

522. Has trace of defects been initiated?

523. Can visual measures help you to filter visualizations of interest?

524. What are you trying to accomplish?

525. Where is quality now?

526. Were quality attributes reported?

527. What method of measurement do you use?

528. Is there a set of procedures to capture, analyze and act on quality metrics?

529. What makes a visualization memorable?

530. Did evaluation start on time?

531. Has it met internal or external standards?

532. Which are the right metrics to use?

533. How do you measure?

534. Were number of defects identified?

535. What about still open problems?

536. What do you measure?

537. What is the benchmark?

538. Who is willing to lead?

539. Do you know how much profit a 10% decrease in waste would generate?

540. Why is now the time for quality metrics?

2.26 Process Improvement Plan: Leadership Styles

541. Where do you want to be?

542. How do you manage quality?

543. What personnel are the change agents for your initiative?

544. Does your process ensure quality?

545. Are there forms and procedures to collect and record the data?

546. What personnel are the sponsors for that initiative?

547. Are you making progress on the goals?

548. Where do you focus?

549. Has the time line required to move measurement results from the points of collection to databases or users been established?

550. What is quality and how will you ensure it?

551. Have the supporting tools been developed or acquired?

552. To elicit goal statements, do you ask a question such as, What do you want to achieve?

553. Are you following the quality standards?

554. If a process improvement framework is being used, which elements will help the problems and goals listed?

555. What lessons have you learned so far?

556. Are you making progress on the improvement framework?

557. Who should prepare the process improvement action plan?

558. What personnel are the coaches for your initiative?

2.27 Responsibility Assignment Matrix: Leadership Styles

559. Does the contractors system provide unit or lot costs when applicable?

560. Do you need to convince people that its well worth the time and effort?

561. Is budgeted cost for work performed calculated in a manner consistent with the way work is planned?

562. How can this help you with team building?

563. Changes in the current direct and Leadership Styles projected base?

564. Will too many Communicating responsibilities tangle the Leadership Styles project in unnecessary communications?

565. Direct labor dollars and/or hours?

566. How do you manage human resources?

567. What is the business need?

568. What is the justification?

569. Does the accounting system provide a basis for auditing records of direct costs chargeable to the contract?

570. Are there any drawbacks to using a responsibility assignment matrix?

571. Are authorized changes being incorporated in a timely manner?

572. What does wbs accomplish?

573. Is accountability placed at the lowest-possible level within the Leadership Styles project so that decisions can be made at that level?

574. Are indirect costs charged to the appropriate indirect pools and incurring organization?

575. What expertise is available in your department?

576. Too many as: does a proper segregation of duties exist?

577. Availability – will the group or the person be available within the necessary time interval?

2.28 Roles and Responsibilities: Leadership Styles

578. Have you ever been a part of this team?

579. What specific behaviors did you observe?

580. Implementation of actions: Who are the responsible units?

581. Attainable / achievable: the goal is attainable; can you actually accomplish the goal?

582. How well did the Leadership Styles project Team understand the expectations of specific roles and responsibilities?

583. Does the team have access to and ability to use data analysis tools?

584. Where are you most strong as a supervisor?

585. Are governance roles and responsibilities documented?

586. Concern: where are you limited or have no authority, where you can not influence?

587. Is the data complete?

588. Once the responsibilities are defined for the Leadership Styles project, have the deliverables, roles and responsibilities been clearly communicated to

every participant?

589. Influence: what areas of organizational decision making are you able to influence when you do not have authority to make the final decision?

590. What is working well within your organizations performance management system?

591. What expectations were NOT met?

592. What areas would you highlight for changes or improvements?

593. Are Leadership Styles project team roles and responsibilities identified and documented?

594. Who: who is involved?

595. Who is responsible for implementation activities and where will the functions, roles and responsibilities be defined?

596. What is working well?

2.29 Human Resource Management Plan: Leadership Styles

597. Has a provision been made to reassess Leadership Styles project risks at various Leadership Styles project stages?

598. Have Leadership Styles project team accountabilities & responsibilities been clearly defined?

599. Is there a formal process for updating the Leadership Styles project baseline?

600. Have adequate resources been provided by management to ensure Leadership Styles project success?

601. Have all involved Leadership Styles project stakeholders and work groups committed to the Leadership Styles project?

602. Do Leadership Styles project managers participating in the Leadership Styles project know the Leadership Styles projects true status first hand?

603. Are decisions captured in a decisions log?

604. Has the schedule been baselined?

605. Have lessons learned been conducted after each Leadership Styles project release?

606. Leadership Styles project definition & scope?

607. Has a quality assurance plan been developed for the Leadership Styles project?

608. Are multiple estimation methods being employed?

609. Measurable - are the targets measurable?

610. Has the budget been baselined?

611. Have all documents been archived in a Leadership Styles project repository for each release?

612. What is this Leadership Styles project aiming to achieve?

613. Timeline and milestones?

614. Are Leadership Styles project team members committed fulltime?

2.30 Communications Management Plan: Leadership Styles

615. How often do you engage with stakeholders?

616. What communications method?

617. Who is involved as you identify stakeholders?

618. Who did you turn to if you had questions?

619. Are stakeholders internal or external?

620. How much time does it take to do it?

621. How is this initiative related to other portfolios, programs, or Leadership Styles projects?

622. Are others part of the communications management plan?

623. Timing: when do the effects of the communication take place?

624. What is the stakeholders level of authority?

625. What to know?

626. Do you have members of your team responsible for certain stakeholders?

627. Do you feel more overwhelmed by stakeholders?

628. Can you think of other people who might have concerns or interests?

629. Who to share with?

630. What does the stakeholder need from the team?

631. Who to learn from?

632. Are you constantly rushing from meeting to meeting?

633. How were corresponding initiatives successful?

2.31 Risk Management Plan: Leadership Styles

634. What things might go wrong?

635. Are some people working on multiple Leadership Styles projects?

636. Why do you want risk management?

637. Is the necessary data being captured and is it complete and accurate?

638. How is risk monitoring performed?

639. Is there additional information that would make you more confident about your analysis?

640. How are risk analysis and prioritization performed?

641. Can the risk be avoided by choosing a different alternative?

642. Has something like this been done before?

643. Do benefits and chances of success outweigh potential damage if success is not attained?

644. Do end-users have realistic expectations?

645. User involvement: do you have the right users?

646. What are the chances the risk event will occur?

647. Is the process supported by tools?

648. How do you manage Leadership Styles project Risk?

649. Are team members trained in the use of the tools?

650. Where are you confronted with risks during the business phases?

2.32 Risk Register: Leadership Styles

651. What are the major risks facing the Leadership Styles project?

652. What action, if any, has been taken to respond to the risk?

653. Are corrective measures implemented as planned?

654. Cost/benefit – how much will the proposed mitigations cost and how does this cost compare with the potential cost of the risk event/situation should it occur?

655. What will be done?

656. Are there any knock-on effects/impact on any of the other areas?

657. Having taken action, how did the responses effect change, and where is the Leadership Styles project now?

658. Who needs to know about this?

659. Who is accountable?

660. What further options might be available for responding to the risk?

661. Assume the event happens, what is the Most Likely impact?

662. Who is going to do it?

663. Schedule impact/severity estimated range (workdays) assume the event happens, what is the potential impact?

664. What are the main aims, objectives of the policy, strategy, or service and the intended outcomes?

665. Budget and schedule: what are the estimated costs and schedules for performing risk-related activities?

666. What are your key risks/show istoppers and what is being done to manage them?

667. What are the assumptions and current status that support the assessment of the risk?

668. What may happen or not go according to plan?

669. What can be done about it?

2.33 Probability and Impact Assessment: Leadership Styles

670. Risk urgency assessment -which of your risks could occur soon, or require a longer planning time?

671. Have you ascribed a level of confidence to every critical technical objective?

672. How would you assess the risk management process in the Leadership Styles project?

673. Will new information become available during the Leadership Styles project?

674. Have customers been involved fully in the definition of requirements?

675. How are you working with risks?

676. Do requirements demand the use of new analysis, design, or testing methods?

677. What is the experience (performance, attitude, business ethics, etc.) in the past with contractors?

678. Are there new risks that mitigation strategies might introduce?

679. Can this technology be absorbed with current level of expertise available in your organization?

680. Anticipated volatility of the requirements?

681. What can you do to minimize the impact if it does?

682. Have top software and customer managers formally committed to support the Leadership Styles project?

683. Will there be an increase in the political conservatism?

684. Are there alternative opinions/solutions/processes you should explore?

685. What is the likely future demand of the customer?

686. Are trained personnel, including supervisors and Leadership Styles project managers, available to handle such a large Leadership Styles project?

687. Are there any Leadership Styles projects similar to this one in existence?

688. Assumptions analysis -what assumptions have you made or been given about your Leadership Styles project?

2.34 Probability and Impact Matrix: Leadership Styles

689. How will the consumption pattern change?

690. How much is the probability of the risk occurring?

691. Have you worked with the customer in the past?

692. What changes in the regulation are forthcoming?

693. What are the likely future requirements?

694. What is the likelihood?

695. What is the probability of the risk occurring?

696. What will be the likely incidence of conflict with neighboring Leadership Styles projects?

697. Maximize short-term return on investment?

698. Are compilers and code generators available and suitable for the product to be built?

699. The customer requests a change to the Leadership Styles project that would increase the Leadership Styles project risk. Which should you do before ass the others?

700. How are the local factors going to affect the absorption?

701. Can you handle the investment risk?

702. Are tools for analysis and design available?

703. What can possibly go wrong?

704. What should be done with risks on the watch list?

705. Workarounds are determined during which step of risk management?

706. What do you expect?

707. Who has experience with this?

708. Is the number of people on the Leadership Styles project team adequate to do the job?

2.35 Risk Data Sheet: Leadership Styles

709. What if client refuses?

710. Potential for recurrence?

711. How do you handle product safely?

712. What are the main threats to your existence?

713. How reliable is the data source?

714. Has a sensitivity analysis been carried out?

715. Type of risk identified?

716. During work activities could hazards exist?

717. What are you weak at and therefore need to do better?

718. Whom do you serve (customers)?

719. How can hazards be reduced?

720. What do you know?

721. If it happens, what are the consequences?

722. What are you here for (Mission)?

723. How can it happen?

724. What are the main opportunities available to you that you should grab while you can?

725. What was measured?

726. Risk of what?

727. Has the most cost-effective solution been chosen?

728. What are you trying to achieve (Objectives)?

2.36 Procurement Management Plan: Leadership Styles

729. Has your organization readiness assessment been conducted?

730. Does the Leadership Styles project have a Quality Culture?

731. Is the schedule updated on a periodic basis?

732. Have Leadership Styles project team accountabilities & responsibilities been clearly defined?

733. Are post milestone Leadership Styles project reviews (PMPR) conducted with your organization at least once a year?

734. Have all unresolved risks been documented?

735. Are procurement deliverables arriving on time and to specification?

736. Based on your Leadership Styles project communication management plan, what worked well?

737. Were Leadership Styles project team members involved in detailed estimating and scheduling?

738. Are all payments made according to the contract(s)?

739. Does the resource management plan include a personnel development plan?

740. Has the Leadership Styles project manager been identified?

741. Was an original risk assessment/risk management plan completed?

742. Does the Leadership Styles project have a formal Leadership Styles project Charter?

743. Are estimating assumptions and constraints captured?

744. Are non-critical path items updated and agreed upon with the teams?

2.37 Source Selection Criteria: Leadership Styles

745. How are clarifications and communications appropriately used?

746. Is the contracting office likely to receive more purchase requests for this item or service during the coming year?

747. Have all evaluators been trained?

748. Team leads: what is your process for assigning ratings?

749. When is it appropriate to issue a DRFP?

750. What procedures are followed when a contractor requires access to classified information or a significant quantity of special material/information?

751. Can you prevent comparison of proposals?

752. With the rapid changes in information technology, will media be readable in five or ten years?

753. How do you facilitate evaluation against published criteria?

754. What documentation is necessary regarding electronic communications?

755. Are types/quantities of material, facilities appropriate?

756. What past performance information should be requested?

757. What will you use to capture evaluation and subsequent documentation?

758. What management structure does your organization consider as optimal for performing the contract?

759. What should a DRFP include?

760. Are there any specific considerations that precludes offers from being selected as the awardee?

761. How should the oral presentations be handled?

762. What source selection software is your team using?

763. How do you ensure an integrated assessment of proposals?

2.38 Stakeholder Management Plan: Leadership Styles

764. Have all involved Leadership Styles project stakeholders and work groups committed to the Leadership Styles project?

765. Where to get additional help?

766. Has a Leadership Styles project Communications Plan been developed?

767. Have all documents been archived in a Leadership Styles project repository for each release?

768. Are all key components of a Quality Assurance Plan present?

769. Contradictory information between different documents?

770. Is a stakeholder management plan in place?

771. Do Leadership Styles project managers participating in the Leadership Styles project know the Leadership Styles projects true status first hand?

772. Is the Leadership Styles project sponsor clearly communicating the business case or rationale for why this Leadership Styles project is needed?

773. Is the communication plan being followed?

774. Has the Leadership Styles project manager been identified?

775. Have activity relationships and interdependencies within tasks been adequately identified?

776. Have all involved stakeholders and work groups committed to the Leadership Styles project?

777. Have Leadership Styles project success criteria been defined?

778. Will the current technology alter during the life of the Leadership Styles project?

779. Are milestone deliverables effectively tracked and compared to Leadership Styles project plan?

780. Where are the verification requirements to be documented (eg purchase order, agreement etc)?

781. How will you engage this stakeholder and gain commitment?

2.39 Change Management Plan: Leadership Styles

782. Who will be the change levers?

783. Readiness -what is a successful end state?

784. What is the most positive interpretation it can receive?

785. Is it the same for each of the business units?

786. How much change management is needed?

787. Who will fund the training?

788. How might they respond to the message and if the response may be negative or open to misinterpretation, what else needs to be said?

789. Are there resource implications for your communications strategy?

790. How will the stakeholders share information and transfer knowledge?

791. What are the specific target groups / audience that will be impacted by this change?

792. Identify the current level of skills and knowledge and behaviours of the group that will be impacted on. What prerequisite knowledge do corresponding groups need?

793. What policies and procedures need to be changed?

794. What are the specific target groups/audiences that will be impacted by this change?

795. What are the essentials of the message?

796. Is there a need for new relationships to be built?

797. Who is the target audience of the piece of information?

798. What are the needs, priorities and special interests of the audience?

799. Have the business unit contacts been briefed by the Leadership Styles project team?

800. Do there need to be new channels developed?

3.0 Executing Process Group: Leadership Styles

801. How many different communication channels does the Leadership Styles project team have?

802. What is the difference between conceptual, application, and evaluative questions?

803. What are deliverables of your Leadership Styles project?

804. How could stakeholders negatively impact your Leadership Styles project?

805. Will additional funds be needed for hardware or software?

806. Do your results resemble a normal distribution?

807. Do the products created live up to the necessary quality?

808. What areas were overlooked on this Leadership Styles project?

809. In what way has the program come up with innovative measures for problem-solving?

810. What Leadership Styles projects and services are in the portfolio of your organization?

811. Is the schedule for the set products being met?

812. It under budget or over budget?

813. Does software appear easy to learn?

814. How do you measure difficulty?

815. What are the typical Leadership Styles project management skills?

816. Based on your Leadership Styles project communication management plan, what worked well?

817. Will new hardware or software be required for servers or client machines?

818. Does the case present a realistic scenario?

819. How well defined and documented were the Leadership Styles project management processes you chose to use?

820. Are escalated issues resolved promptly?

3.1 Team Member Status Report: Leadership Styles

821. How it is to be done?

822. Does every department have to have a Leadership Styles project Manager on staff?

823. Does the product, good, or service already exist within your organization?

824. Why is it to be done?

825. Will the staff do training or is that done by a third party?

826. Are your organizations Leadership Styles projects more successful over time?

827. How much risk is involved?

828. Does your organization have the means (staff, money, contract, etc.) to produce or to acquire the product, good, or service?

829. What specific interest groups do you have in place?

830. How will resource planning be done?

831. Are the attitudes of staff regarding Leadership Styles project work improving?

832. The problem with Reward & Recognition Programs is that the truly deserving people all too often get left out. How can you make it practical?

833. What is to be done?

834. How can you make it practical?

835. How does this product, good, or service meet the needs of the Leadership Styles project and your organization as a whole?

836. Is there evidence that staff is taking a more professional approach toward management of your organizations Leadership Styles projects?

837. When a teams productivity and success depend on collaboration and the efficient flow of information, what generally fails them?

838. Do you have an Enterprise Leadership Styles project Management Office (EPMO)?

839. Are the products of your organizations Leadership Styles projects meeting customers objectives?

3.2 Change Request: Leadership Styles

840. Who is included in the change control team?

841. Should staff call into the helpdesk or go to the website?

842. How is the change documented (format, content, storage)?

843. How are changes graded and who is responsible for the rating?

844. What needs to be communicated?

845. How are the measures for carrying out the change established?

846. Will new change requests be acknowledged in a timely manner?

847. What is the function of the change control committee?

848. What type of changes does change control take into account?

849. What has an inspector to inspect and to check?

850. Will all change requests be unconditionally tracked through this process?

851. Has the change been highlighted and documented in the CSCI?

852. How do you get changes (code) out in a timely manner?

853. For which areas does this operating procedure apply?

854. How do team members communicate with each other?

855. How is quality being addressed on the Leadership Styles project?

856. Who has responsibility for approving and ranking changes?

857. Change request coordination ?

858. Will the change use memory to the extent that other functions will be not have sufficient memory to operate effectively?

859. What can be filed?

3.3 Change Log: Leadership Styles

860. When was the request approved?

861. When was the request submitted?

862. Is the requested change request a result of changes in other Leadership Styles project(s)?

863. Is the change backward compatible without limitations?

864. Who initiated the change request?

865. Should a more thorough impact analysis be conducted?

866. Is the submitted change a new change or a modification of a previously approved change?

867. Does the suggested change request represent a desired enhancement to the products functionality?

868. Does the suggested change request seem to represent a necessary enhancement to the product?

869. How does this change affect scope?

870. How does this change affect the timeline of the schedule?

871. Is this a mandatory replacement?

872. Is the change request within Leadership Styles

project scope?

873. How does this relate to the standards developed for specific business processes?

874. Will the Leadership Styles project fail if the change request is not executed?

875. Where do changes come from?

876. Do the described changes impact on the integrity or security of the system?

877. Is the change request open, closed or pending?

3.4 Decision Log: Leadership Styles

878. What is your overall strategy for quality control / quality assurance procedures?

879. What is the line where eDiscovery ends and document review begins?

880. How does provision of information, both in terms of content and presentation, influence acceptance of alternative strategies?

881. Who is the decisionmaker?

882. What are the cost implications?

883. Meeting purpose; why does this team meet?

884. At what point in time does loss become unacceptable?

885. Linked to original objective?

886. Behaviors; what are guidelines that the team has identified that will assist them with getting the most out of team meetings?

887. Is your opponent open to a non-traditional workflow, or will it likely challenge anything you do?

888. Is everything working as expected?

889. How does the use a Decision Support System influence the strategies/tactics or costs?

890. What was the rationale for the decision?

891. What makes you different or better than others companies selling the same thing?

892. Who will be given a copy of this document and where will it be kept?

893. Decision-making process; how will the team make decisions?

894. With whom was the decision shared or considered?

895. Do strategies and tactics aimed at less than full control reduce the costs of management or simply shift the cost burden?

896. How consolidated and comprehensive a story can you tell by capturing currently available incident data in a central location and through a log of key decisions during an incident?

897. How effective is maintaining the log at facilitating organizational learning?

3.5 Quality Audit: Leadership Styles

898. What review processes are in place for your organizations major activities?

899. How does your organization know that it is appropriately effective and constructive in preparing its staff for organizational aspirations?

900. Is quality audit a prerequisite for program accreditation or program recognition?

901. How does your organization know that its relationship with its (past) staff is appropriately effective and constructive?

902. What is your organizations greatest strength?

903. How does the organization know that its industry and community engagement planning and management systems are appropriately effective and constructive in enabling relationships with key stakeholder groups?

904. Are there appropriate means for intervening if necessary?

905. Are all staff empowered and encouraged to contribute to ongoing improvement efforts?

906. Are training programs documented?

907. How do you know what, specifically, is required of you in your work?

908. How does your organization know that it is maintaining a conducive staff climate?

909. Does your organization have set of goals, objectives, strategies and targets that are clearly understood by the Board and staff?

910. If your organization thinks it is doing something well, can it prove this?

911. Are salvageable and salvaged medical devices stored in a manner to prevent damage and/or contamination?

912. Do prior clients have a positive opinion of your organization?

913. How does your organization know that its relationships with the community at large are appropriately effective and constructive?

914. How does your organization know that its system for managing intellectual property issues is appropriately effective, constructive and fair?

915. How does your organization know that the support for its staff is appropriately effective and constructive?

916. What are you trying to accomplish with this audit?

917. Will the evidence likely be sufficient and appropriate?

3.6 Team Directory: Leadership Styles

918. Process decisions: do invoice amounts match accepted work in place?

919. Process decisions: how well was task order work performed?

920. Who will talk to the customer?

921. What are you going to deliver or accomplish?

922. Who will be the stakeholders on your next Leadership Styles project?

923. When will you produce deliverables?

924. Process decisions: are all start-up, turn over and close out requirements of the contract satisfied?

925. Process decisions: which organizational elements and which individuals will be assigned management functions?

926. Who are your stakeholders (customers, sponsors, end users, team members)?

927. Does a Leadership Styles project team directory list all resources assigned to the Leadership Styles project?

928. Days from the time the issue is identified?

929. Process decisions: is work progressing on

schedule and per contract requirements?

930. Who is the Sponsor?

931. How do unidentified risks impact the outcome of the Leadership Styles project?

932. Timing: when do the effects of communication take place?

933. Contract requirements complied with?

934. How does the team resolve conflicts and ensure tasks are completed?

935. How and in what format should information be presented?

936. Who are the Team Members?

3.7 Team Operating Agreement: Leadership Styles

937. How do you want to be thought of and known within your organization?

938. What is the anticipated procedure (recruitment, solicitation of volunteers, or assignment) for selecting team members?

939. Did you recap the meeting purpose, time, and expectations?

940. Do you post meeting notes and the recording (if used) and notify participants?

941. Are there the right people on your team?

942. Do you vary your voice pace, tone and pitch to engage participants and gain involvement?

943. Resource allocation: how will individual team members account for time and expenses, and how will this be allocated in the team budget?

944. Are there differences in access to communication and collaboration technology based on team member location?

945. Did you prepare participants for the next meeting?

946. What is group supervision?

947. To whom do you deliver your services?

948. Are leadership responsibilities shared among team members (versus a single leader)?

949. What are the safety issues/risks that need to be addressed and/or that the team needs to consider?

950. What is culture?

951. What are the current caseload numbers in the unit?

952. Reimbursements: how will the team members be reimbursed for expenses and time commitments?

953. Do you ensure that all participants know how to use the required technology?

954. Did you delegate tasks such as taking meeting minutes, presenting a topic and soliciting input?

955. Does your team need access to all documents and information at all times?

956. Must your members collaborate successfully to complete Leadership Styles projects?

3.8 Team Performance Assessment: Leadership Styles

957. What are you doing specifically to develop the leaders around you?

958. To what degree is the team cognizant of small wins to be celebrated along the way?

959. What do you think is the most constructive thing that could be done now to resolve considerations and disputes about method variance?

960. To what degree does the teams work approach provide opportunity for members to engage in results-based evaluation?

961. To what degree are the members clear on what they are individually responsible for and what they are jointly responsible for?

962. How does Leadership Styles project termination impact Leadership Styles project team members?

963. To what degree will team members, individually and collectively, commit time to help themselves and others learn and develop skills?

964. To what degree does the teams work approach provide opportunity for members to engage in open interaction?

965. To what degree do team members understand

one anothers roles and skills?

966. To what degree will the team ensure that all members equitably share the work essential to the success of the team?

967. To what degree do team members frequently explore the teams purpose and its implications?

968. When does the medium matter?

969. To what degree will the approach capitalize on and enhance the skills of all team members in a manner that takes into consideration other demands on members of the team?

970. To what degree are staff involved as partners in the improvement process?

971. If you have criticized someones work for method variance in your role as reviewer, what was the circumstance?

972. To what degree are the goals ambitious?

973. To what degree will the team adopt a concrete, clearly understood, and agreed-upon approach that will result in achievement of the teams goals?

974. Does more radicalness mean more perceived benefits?

975. What are teams?

976. How hard did you try to make a good selection?

3.9 Team Member Performance Assessment: Leadership Styles

977. Who should attend?

978. What is the role of the Reviewer?

979. To what extent are systems and applications (e.g., game engine, mobile device platform) utilized?

980. Are the draft goals SMART ?

981. How do you currently use the time that is available?

982. To what degree does the teams purpose contain themes that are particularly meaningful and memorable?

983. To what degree are the skill areas critical to team performance present?

984. To what degree do all members feel responsible for all agreed-upon measures?

985. How do you make use of research?

986. To what degree can team members meet frequently enough to accomplish the teams ends?

987. What innovations (if any) are developed to realize goals?

988. Are the goals SMART?

989. What are best practices in use for the performance measurement system?

990. Did training work?

991. Verify business objectives. Are they appropriate, and well-articulated?

992. How is assessment information achieved, stored?

993. Which training platform formats (i.e., mobile, virtual, videogame-based) were implemented in your effort(s)?

994. What stakeholders must be involved in the development and oversight of the performance plan?

995. What is a significant fact or event?

3.10 Issue Log: Leadership Styles

996. What is the impact on the risks?

997. Persistence; will users learn a work around or will they be bothered every time?

998. What would have to change?

999. Is access to the Issue Log controlled?

1000. What approaches do you use?

1001. What date was the issue resolved?

1002. Are the Leadership Styles project issues uniquely identified, including to which product they refer?

1003. Is the issue log kept in a safe place?

1004. Which stakeholders are thought leaders, influences, or early adopters?

1005. Are there common objectives between the team and the stakeholder?

1006. Who is the issue assigned to?

1007. What approaches to you feel are the best ones to use?

1008. What are the typical contents?

1009. What is a Stakeholder?

1010. Who do you turn to if you have questions?

1011. Who were proponents/opponents?

1012. Why do you manage communications?

4.0 Monitoring and Controlling Process Group: Leadership Styles

1013. Do the partners have sufficient financial capacity to keep up the benefits produced by the programme?

1014. How well did the chosen processes produce the expected results?

1015. What kinds of things in particular are you looking for data on?

1016. Did the Leadership Styles project team have enough people to execute the Leadership Styles project plan?

1017. How well did the team follow the chosen processes?

1018. How well defined and documented were the Leadership Styles project management processes you chose to use?

1019. Does the solution fit in with organizations technical architectural requirements?

1020. What resources (both financial and non-financial) are available/needed?

1021. Use: how will they use the information?

1022. Feasibility: how much money, time, and effort

can you put into this?

1023. Did the Leadership Styles project team have the right skills?

1024. Is there undesirable impact on staff or resources?

1025. What do they need to know about the Leadership Styles project?

1026. Is there sufficient funding available for this?

1027. How is agile portfolio management done?

4.1 Project Performance Report: Leadership Styles

1028. What is in it for you?

1029. To what degree can all members engage in open and interactive considerations?

1030. To what degree does the information network provide individuals with the information they require?

1031. To what degree are sub-teams possible or necessary?

1032. To what degree can the team ensure that all members are individually and jointly accountable for the teams purpose, goals, approach, and work-products?

1033. To what degree does the funding match the requirement?

1034. What is the degree to which rules govern information exchange between groups?

1035. To what degree will new and supplemental skills be introduced as the need is recognized?

1036. To what degree do the relationships of the informal organization motivate taskrelevant behavior and facilitate task completion?

1037. To what degree are the demands of the task

compatible with and converge with the mission and functions of the formal organization?

1038. To what degree does the information network communicate information relevant to the task?

1039. How is the data used?

1040. How can Leadership Styles project sustainability be maintained?

1041. To what degree do team members articulate the teams work approach?

1042. To what degree can the cognitive capacity of individuals accommodate the flow of information?

4.2 Variance Analysis: Leadership Styles

1043. Are meaningful indicators identified for use in measuring the status of cost and schedule performance?

1044. What is the dollar amount of the fluctuation?

1045. Does the contractors system identify work accomplishment against the schedule plan?

1046. What is the incurrence of actual indirect costs in excess of budgets, by element of expense?

1047. Are the overhead pools formally and adequately identified?

1048. How do you manage changes in the nature of the overhead requirements?

1049. Is the entire contract planned in time-phased control accounts to the extent practicable?

1050. Are the bases and rates for allocating costs from each indirect pool consistently applied?

1051. Are procedures for variance analysis documented and consistently applied at the control account level and selected WBS and organizational levels at least monthly as a routine task?

1052. What should management do?

1053. Budgeted cost for work performed?

1054. Are all budgets assigned to control accounts?

1055. Are control accounts opened and closed based on the start and completion of work contained therein?

1056. What is exceptional?

1057. Who is generally responsible for monitoring and taking action on variances?

1058. How does the use of a single conversion element (rather than the traditional labor and overhead elements) affect standard costing?

1059. Are there changes in the overhead pool and/or organization structures?

1060. Does the contractor use objective results, design reviews and tests to trace schedule performance?

1061. What business event causes fluctuations?

1062. There are detailed schedules which support control account and work package start and completion dates/events?

4.3 Earned Value Status: Leadership Styles

1063. Where are your problem areas?

1064. When is it going to finish?

1065. How does this compare with other Leadership Styles projects?

1066. Earned value can be used in almost any Leadership Styles project situation and in almost any Leadership Styles project environment. it may be used on large Leadership Styles projects, medium sized Leadership Styles projects, tiny Leadership Styles projects (in cut-down form), complex and simple Leadership Styles projects and in any market sector. some people, of course, know all about earned value, they have used it for years - but perhaps not as effectively as they could have?

1067. Are you hitting your Leadership Styles projects targets?

1068. How much is it going to cost by the finish?

1069. Verification is a process of ensuring that the developed system satisfies the stakeholders agreements and specifications; Are you building the product right? What do you verify?

1070. Validation is a process of ensuring that the developed system will actually achieve the stakeholders desired outcomes; Are you building the right product? What do you validate?

1071. If earned value management (EVM) is so good in determining the true status of a Leadership Styles project and Leadership Styles project its completion, why is it that hardly any one uses it in information systems related Leadership Styles projects?

1072. What is the unit of forecast value?

1073. Where is evidence-based earned value in your organization reported?

4.4 Risk Audit: Leadership Styles

1074. Strategic business risk audit methodologies; are corresponding an attempt to sell other services, and is management becoming the client of the audit rather than the shareholder?

1075. Are there any forms the staff is required to sign?

1076. Are procedures developed to respond to foreseeable emergencies and communicated to all involved?

1077. Is there a clear procedure for reporting accidents/injuries?

1078. Is all required equipment available?

1079. What are the costs associated with late delivery or a defective product?

1080. Is the technology to be built new to your organization?

1081. What responsibilities for quality, errors, and outcomes have been delegated to staff (or others) without adequate oversight?

1082. Is your organization an exempt employer for payroll tax purposes?

1083. Are testing tools available and suitable?

1084. Are end-users enthusiastically committed to the

Leadership Styles project and the system/product to be built?

1085. Estimated size of product in number of programs, files, transactions?

1086. Does the implementation method matter?

1087. If applicable; are compilers and code generators available and suitable for the product to be built?

1088. How do you govern assets?

1089. What expertise do auditors need to generate effective business-level risk assessments, and to what extent do auditors currently possess the already stated attributes?

1090. Auditor independence: a burdensome constraint or a core value?

1091. Level of preparation and skill?

1092. Are all participants informed of safety issues?

1093. Have all possible risks/hazards been identified (including injury to staff, damage to equipment, impact on others in the community)?

4.5 Contractor Status Report: Leadership Styles

1094. What process manages the contracts?

1095. What are the minimum and optimal bandwidth requirements for the proposed solution?

1096. How long have you been using the services?

1097. Are there contractual transfer concerns?

1098. What was the final actual cost?

1099. Who can list a Leadership Styles project as organization experience, your organization or a previous employee of your organization?

1100. What is the average response time for answering a support call?

1101. How is risk transferred?

1102. If applicable; describe your standard schedule for new software version releases. Are new software version releases included in the standard maintenance plan?

1103. What was the actual budget or estimated cost for your organizations services?

1104. What was the overall budget or estimated cost?

1105. Describe how often regular updates are made to the proposed solution. Are corresponding regular updates included in the standard maintenance plan?

1106. What was the budget or estimated cost for your organizations services?

4.6 Formal Acceptance: Leadership Styles

1107. What features, practices, and processes proved to be strengths or weaknesses?

1108. Was the Leadership Styles project goal achieved?

1109. What is the Acceptance Management Process?

1110. Was the Leadership Styles project work done on time, within budget, and according to specification?

1111. What was done right?

1112. Did the Leadership Styles project manager and team act in a professional and ethical manner?

1113. Was the sponsor/customer satisfied?

1114. Is formal acceptance of the Leadership Styles project product documented and distributed?

1115. Do you buy pre-configured systems or build your own configuration?

1116. What can you do better next time?

1117. Does it do what client said it would?

1118. General estimate of the costs and times to complete the Leadership Styles project?

1119. Who supplies data?

1120. How does your team plan to obtain formal acceptance on your Leadership Styles project?

1121. What are the requirements against which to test, Who will execute?

1122. Do you buy-in installation services?

1123. Was the Leadership Styles project managed well?

1124. What lessons were learned about your Leadership Styles project management methodology?

1125. Who would use it?

1126. What function(s) does it fill or meet?

5.0 Closing Process Group: Leadership Styles

1127. Contingency planning. if a risk event occurs, what will you do?

1128. Were the outcomes different from the already stated planned?

1129. How well defined and documented were the Leadership Styles project management processes you chose to use?

1130. What is the Leadership Styles project Management Process?

1131. What was learned?

1132. Did the delivered product meet the specified requirements and goals of the Leadership Styles project?

1133. How well did the chosen processes fit the needs of the Leadership Styles project?

1134. What areas were overlooked on this Leadership Styles project?

1135. 'What were things that you did very well and want to do the same again on the next Leadership Styles project?

1136. What were things that you need to improve?

1137. Who are the Leadership Styles project stakeholders?

1138. If a risk event occurs, what will you do?

1139. What is the Leadership Styles project name and date of completion?

1140. Did the Leadership Styles project management methodology work?

1141. What were the actual outcomes?

1142. Does the close educate others to improve performance?

1143. Just how important is your work to the overall success of the Leadership Styles project?

5.1 Procurement Audit: Leadership Styles

1144. Budget controls: does your organization maintain an up-to-date (approved) budget for all funded activities, and perform a comparison of that budget with actual expenditures for each budget category?

1145. Did the additional works introduce minor or non-substantial changes to performance, as described in the contract documents?

1146. Has the department identified and described the different elements in the procurement process?

1147. When tenders were actually rejected because they were abnormally low, were reasons for this decision given and were they sufficiently grounded?

1148. Which are necessary components of a financial audit report under the Single Audit Act?

1149. When performance conditions were detailed in the tender documentation, did the contracting authority verify if the tenders received met the already stated requirements?

1150. Have the funding arrangements been agreed where payments take place over several financial periods?

1151. Does the cash disbursement policy prohibit

drawing checks to cash or bearer?

1152. Were no charges billed to interested economic operators or the parties to the system?

1153. Do staff involved in the various stages of the process have the appropriate skills and training to perform duties effectively?

1154. Was the chosen procedure the most efficient and effective for the performance of the contract?

1155. Are there procedures governing how sales and use tax will be handled (ordering in state versus ordering out of state)?

1156. Is there no evidence of any individual on the evaluation panel being biased?

1157. Are there policies regarding special approval for capital expenditures?

1158. Are copies of policies made available to staff members involved in budget preparation and administration?

1159. Was the decision on the award process accurate and adequately communicated?

1160. Is funding made available for payments under the contract at the appropriate time and in accordance with the relevant national/public financial procedures?

1161. Were the documents received scrutinised for completion and adherence to stated conditions before the tenders were evaluated?

1162. Are all checks stored in a secure area?

1163. Did your organization state the minimum requirements to be met by the variants in the tender documents?

5.2 Contract Close-Out: Leadership Styles

1164. Change in circumstances?

1165. Have all acceptance criteria been met prior to final payment to contractors?

1166. Was the contract complete without requiring numerous changes and revisions?

1167. What happens to the recipient of services?

1168. What is capture management?

1169. Was the contract sufficiently clear so as not to result in numerous disputes and misunderstandings?

1170. How does it work?

1171. Parties: Authorized?

1172. Have all contracts been closed?

1173. How is the contracting office notified of the automatic contract close-out?

1174. How/when used ?

1175. Change in attitude or behavior?

1176. Are the signers the authorized officials?

1177. Was the contract type appropriate?

1178. Why Outsource?

1179. Have all contract records been included in the Leadership Styles project archives?

1180. Have all contracts been completed?

1181. Change in knowledge?

1182. Has each contract been audited to verify acceptance and delivery?

1183. Parties: who is involved?

5.3 Project or Phase Close-Out: Leadership Styles

1184. Who controlled the resources for the Leadership Styles project?

1185. Did the delivered product meet the specified requirements and goals of the Leadership Styles project?

1186. Complete yes or no?

1187. Which changes might a stakeholder be required to make as a result of the Leadership Styles project?

1188. Can the lesson learned be replicated?

1189. Did the Leadership Styles project management methodology work?

1190. What information did each stakeholder need to contribute to the Leadership Styles projects success?

1191. Was the schedule met?

1192. What could be done to improve the process?

1193. In addition to assessing whether the Leadership Styles project was successful, it is equally critical to analyze why it was or was not fully successful. Are you including this?

1194. What can you do better next time, and what

specific actions can you take to improve?

1195. What is a Risk?

1196. Planned completion date?

1197. Who is responsible for award close-out?

1198. What was the preferred delivery mechanism?

1199. What information is each stakeholder group interested in?

1200. What advantages do the an individual interview have over a group meeting, and vice-versa?

1201. What is this stakeholder expecting?

5.4 Lessons Learned: Leadership Styles

1202. What were the key issues?

1203. What is your strategy for data collection?

1204. How long did redeployment take?

1205. How will you allocate your funding resources?

1206. What is your organizations performance history?

1207. Were the right people available when required?

1208. How many interest groups are stakeholders?

1209. What mistakes did you successfully avoid making?

1210. Did the Leadership Styles project improve the team members reputations, skills, personal development?

1211. Was sufficient advance training conducted and/or information provided to enable the already stated affected by the changes to adjust to and accommodate them?

1212. What are the performance measures?

1213. What were the lessons learned on this

Leadership Styles project?

1214. Was any formal risk assessment carried out at the start of the Leadership Styles project, and was this followed up during the Leadership Styles project?

1215. What should have been accomplished during predeployment that was not accomplished?

1216. What worked well?

1217. How well prepared were you to receive Leadership Styles project deliverables?

1218. How effective was the acceptance management process?

1219. What things surprised you on the Leadership Styles project that were not in the plan?

1220. How effective was the support you received during implementation of the product/service?

1221. What is the growth stage of your organization?

Index

ability 37, 76, 191
abnormally 253
absorbed 201
absorption 203
acceptable 54, 80, 94
acceptance 6, 113, 121, 141, 148, 223, 249-250, 256-257, 261
accepted 138, 141, 227
access 2, 7-9, 20, 62, 156, 191, 209, 229-230, 235
accidents 245
accomplish 7, 79, 104, 116, 131, 160, 185, 190-191, 226-227, 233
accordance 254
according 39, 41, 200, 207, 249
account 37, 48, 219, 229, 241-242
accounting 189
accounts 241-242
accuracy 48, 148
accurate 9, 114, 181, 197, 254
achievable 124, 191
achieve 7, 58, 79, 86, 107, 111, 187, 194, 206, 243
achieved 17, 87, 116, 234, 249
acquire 217
acquired 159, 187
across 52
action 52, 55, 94, 97, 99, 130, 137, 149, 188, 199, 242
actionable 44, 113
actions 25, 51, 93, 96, 106, 137, 155, 177, 191, 259
active 137, 157, 175, 184
activities 18, 21, 25, 38, 78, 90, 94, 118, 136-137, 140, 156, 158-160, 164-165, 168, 171, 173, 177, 192, 200, 205, 225, 253
activity 3-4, 34, 36, 137, 156, 158, 160-162, 164-166, 169, 171, 173-174, 177-178, 212
actual 34, 45, 170, 181, 241, 247, 252-253
actually 30, 69, 85, 98, 184, 191, 243, 253
addition 123, 258
additional 33, 40, 58-59, 61, 65, 179, 197, 211, 215, 253
additions 98
address 15, 75, 132, 173
addressed 166, 220, 230
addressing 37, 107

adequate   38, 151, 183, 193, 204, 245
adequately   40, 212, 241, 254
adherence   254
adjust 96, 99, 260
adjusted   93
adopters   235
advance   260
advantage   58, 123
advantages   115, 162, 259
adverse   155
affect 62, 70, 108, 114, 125-126, 137, 146, 148, 181, 203, 221, 242
affected   131, 141, 260
affecting   11, 16, 70
affordable   82
against 40, 90, 93, 183, 209, 241, 250
agencies   135
agendas   111
agents 187
aggregate   52
agreed   141, 208, 253
agreement   5, 120, 143, 212, 229
agreements   65, 76, 243
agrees 123
aiming 111, 194
alerts   90
aligned   20
Alignment   176
alleged   1
alliance   86
allocate   122, 260
allocated   52, 104, 229
allocating   241
allocation   229
allowable   55
allowed   109, 167-168
allows 9, 174
almost 243
already   118, 183, 217, 246, 251, 253, 260
always 9, 178
ambitious   232
amended   150
amount   15, 241

amounts 227
amplify 66, 124
analvsis 197
analysis 2, 5, 9-10, 61, 66-67, 71, 77-78, 80, 134, 138, 167, 175-176, 180, 191, 197, 201-202, 204-205, 221, 241
analyze 2, 57, 59, 185, 258
analyzed 81, 90
annually 154
another 152, 169
anothers 232
answer 10-11, 15, 27, 43, 57, 73, 89, 102
answered 26, 42, 56, 71, 88, 100, 127
answering 10, 247
anticipate 148
anyone 35, 111
anything 158, 166, 223
appear 1, 216
applicable 10, 92, 144, 189, 246-247
applied 78, 96, 138, 160, 241
appointed 30, 41
appraise 134
approach 53, 75, 82, 103, 115, 123, 218, 231-232, 239-240
approaches 76, 235
approval 39, 106, 254
approvals 142, 151
approve 130, 149
approved 28, 69, 130, 138, 147, 181, 221, 253
approving 146, 220
Architects 7
archived 156, 194, 211
archives 257
around 116, 231, 235
arriving 207
articulate 240
ascribed 201
asking 1, 7
assess 17, 31, 96, 109, 164, 201
assessed 81
assessing 78, 95, 258
assessment 4-5, 8-9, 17, 136, 142, 200-201, 207-208, 210, 231, 233-234, 261
assets 51, 246
assign 21

assigned 29, 148-149, 152, 160, 174, 227, 235, 242
assigning 209
assignment 4, 189-190, 229
assist 8, 60, 87, 179, 223
assistant 7
associated 129, 144, 245
assume 199-200
Assumption 3, 150
assurance 23, 175, 194, 211, 223
attached 172
attainable 34, 170, 191
attained 197
attempt 245
attempted 35
attempting 99
attend 19, 233
attendance 30
attendant 80
attended 30
attention 11, 120
attitude 201, 256
attitudes 217
attribute 150
attributes 3, 105, 160, 185, 246
audience 213-214
audiences 214
audited 257
auditing 22, 96, 108, 189
Auditor 246
auditors 246
author 1
authority 59, 143, 155, 191-192, 195, 253
authorized 139, 141, 154, 190, 256
automatic 256
available 21, 25, 39-40, 65, 68, 85, 107, 129, 139, 154, 159, 164, 190, 199, 201-204, 206, 224, 233, 237-238, 245-246, 254, 260
Average 11, 26, 42, 56, 71, 88, 100, 127, 247
avoided 197
awardee 210
background 9
backward 221
balanced 76
bandwidth 247

barriers 104
baseline   4, 116, 143, 154, 181, 193
baselined   156, 193-194
baselines   29, 39
basically   177
basics 121
bearer 254
because   173, 253
become   107, 117, 121, 141-142, 146, 201, 223
becoming   245
before 9, 35, 100, 141, 158, 164, 171, 197, 203, 255
beginning   2, 14, 26, 42, 56, 71, 88, 101, 127
begins 223
behavior   239, 256
behaviors   24, 53, 191, 223
behaviours   213
belief 10, 15, 27, 43, 57, 73, 89, 102, 105
believable   124
believe 105, 123
benchmark   186
benefit 1, 21-22, 80, 100, 175, 199
benefits   23, 45-46, 48, 65, 68, 102, 111, 113, 116-117, 132, 164, 197, 232, 237
better 7, 40, 43, 87, 135, 158, 171, 179, 205, 224, 249, 258
between   67, 146, 150, 154, 175, 211, 215, 235, 239
biased 254
biggest   53, 81
billed   254
blinding   62
bother 49
bothered   235
bottleneck   159
bounce   60, 71
boundaries   33
bounds   34
Breakdown   3, 85, 137, 152, 167
briefed 41, 214
brings 39
broken 67
brought   149
budget   85, 91, 97, 107, 138, 154, 159, 173, 194, 200, 216, 229, 247-249, 253-254
budgeted   45, 189, 242

budgeting 154
budgets 154-155, 241-242
building 25, 94, 131, 189, 243-244
burden 224
burdensome 246
business 1, 7, 9, 16, 24, 31, 39, 44, 46, 66, 83, 99, 106, 108, 111, 115-116, 118, 120, 124-125, 129, 144, 181, 189, 198, 201, 211, 213-214, 222, 234, 242, 245
buy-in 121, 250
calculated 189
called 130
cannot 154
capability 17, 131, 151
capable 7, 32
capacities 112
capacity 17, 25, 77, 131, 237, 240
capital 110, 254
capitalize 71, 232
capture 44, 91, 185, 210, 256
captured 52, 67, 74, 116, 141, 144, 156, 175, 193, 197, 208
capturing 224
career 146
careers 124
carried 57, 205, 261
carrying 219
caseload 230
category 31, 253
caused 1, 46
causes 45, 47, 55, 57, 64, 67, 70, 93, 136, 139, 242
causing 16
celebrate 78
celebrated 231
center 53
central 224
centrally 76
certain 103, 129, 195
certified 175
challenge 7, 223
challenges 116, 162
chances 197-198
change 5, 15, 18, 35, 48, 54, 61, 69, 71, 78, 81-82, 92, 126, 133, 139, 142-143, 148-149, 176-177, 184, 187, 199, 203, 213-214, 219-222, 235, 256-257

267

changed   24, 35, 84, 89, 94, 140, 178, 180, 214
changes   16, 41, 45, 69, 80, 98, 100, 113, 141, 145, 148-151, 155, 167, 189-190, 192, 203, 209, 219-222, 241-242, 253, 256, 258, 260
changing   96, 116
channels   144, 214-215
chargeable   189
charged   49, 190
charges   254
Charter   2, 33, 38, 76, 131, 208
charts 61, 174
cheaper   43
checked   62, 90, 93, 99, 144
checklists   8, 140
checks 157, 254-255
choice 30, 109
choose   10, 136
choosing   197
chosen 131, 206, 237, 251, 254
circumvent   23
claimed   1
clarify 123
classified   209
clearly 10, 15-16, 27-28, 36, 43, 57, 64, 73, 81, 89, 102, 144, 191, 193, 207, 211, 226, 232
client   46, 113, 138, 205, 216, 245, 249
clients 17, 31, 226
climate   226
closed 99, 175, 222, 242, 256
closely 9
Close-Out   6, 256, 258-259
closest 122
Closing 6, 65, 251
coaches   31, 188
cognitive   240
cognizant   231
colleague   105
colleagues   106, 116
collect 58, 97, 180, 187
collected   33, 40, 58, 61-63, 66, 81, 169
collection   61, 187, 260
coming   209
command   97

commit	231
commitment	96, 154, 212
committed	69, 157, 184, 193-194, 202, 211-212, 245
committee	157, 175, 184, 219
common	149, 178, 235
community	171, 179-180, 225-226, 246
companies	1, 92, 169, 224
company	7, 43, 58, 105, 111, 114, 120, 124, 126
compare	61, 84, 199, 243
compared	104, 141, 170, 181, 183, 212
comparing	76
comparison	10, 209, 253
compatible	221, 240
compelling	29
competing	50
compile	184
compilers	203, 246
complete	1, 8, 10, 18, 30-31, 34, 149, 157, 160, 171, 185, 191, 197, 230, 249, 256, 258
completed	11, 27, 30, 32, 129, 141, 149, 159, 164, 208, 228, 257
completely	118
completing	153, 164
completion	28, 36, 154, 164, 181, 239, 242, 244, 252, 254, 259
complex	7, 105, 139, 173, 243
complexity	53, 55, 67
compliance	16, 47-48, 56, 76, 150-151
complied	228
comply	131
components	150, 211, 253
comprise	136
compute	11
computer	151
computing	118
concept	79, 163
conceptual	215
concern	50, 86, 191
concerned	18
concerns	17, 23, 122, 196, 247
concrete	181, 232
condition	95
conditions	93, 115, 134-135, 253-254
conducive	226

conduct	183-184
conducted	183, 193, 207, 221, 260
confidence	201
confident	197
confirm	10
conflict	203
conflicts	114, 144-145, 173, 228
conform	150
confronted	198
connected	173
connecting	126
consider	15, 23, 25, 131, 160, 177, 210, 230
considered	16, 21, 51, 224
considers	58
consistent	39, 95, 137, 154, 189
constantly	196
Constraint	3, 150, 246
consultant	7
consulted	108
contact	7, 157
contacts	214
contain	18, 65, 99, 138, 233
contained	1, 242
contains	8
content	38, 219, 223
contents	1-2, 8, 235
context	37, 40, 42
continual	98-99
Continuity	44, 162
continuous	68, 78
contract	6, 154, 164, 170, 178, 189, 207, 210, 217, 227-228, 241, 253-254, 256-257
contractor	6, 155, 178, 209, 242, 247
contracts	39, 65, 135, 162, 175, 247, 256-257
contribute	125, 135, 145, 225, 258
control	2, 42, 56, 58, 85, 89, 91-95, 97, 130, 134-135, 138, 142-143, 179, 219, 223-224, 241-242
controlled	65, 235, 258
controls	18, 63, 68, 74, 82, 85, 96-97, 99-100, 164, 253
convention	122
converge	240
conversion	242
convey	1

convince 189
cooperate 179
copies 254
Copyright 1
correct 43, 89
corrected 176
corrective 51, 93, 199
correspond 8-9
costing 242
counter 134
counting 125, 155
counts 125
course 35, 48, 243
covering 8, 90
coworker 113
crashing 164
craziest 121
create 16, 115, 121, 124, 149
created 66, 89, 133, 139-140, 215
creating 7, 53
creative 21
creativity 81
credible 179
crisis 17
criteria 2, 5, 8-9, 29-30, 34, 65, 83, 87, 95, 117, 128, 138, 141, 146, 149, 173, 180, 183, 209, 212, 256
CRITERION 2, 15, 27, 43, 57, 73, 89, 102
critical 36, 38, 40, 66, 79, 96-97, 104, 159, 163, 170, 201, 233, 258
criticized 232
cross-sell 126
crucial 60, 134-135
crystal 10
cultural 116
culture 41, 70, 106, 207, 230
current 29, 43-44, 50, 59, 61, 64, 67, 83-84, 97, 105 120-122, 150, 156, 164, 183, 189, 200-201, 212-213, 230
currently 41, 110, 224, 233, 246
custom 23
customer 25, 28-29, 33, 37, 39-40, 79, 98-99, 102, 105, 111, 119, 132, 145, 181, 202-203, 227, 249
customers 1, 25, 30, 38, 44, 47, 49, 54, 59, 61, 91, 107-108, 110, 113, 115, 117-119, 144, 148, 150, 176, 184, 201, 205, 218, 227
cut-down 243

damage 1, 197, 226, 246
Dashboard 8
dashboards 98
databases 187
day-to-day 98, 126
deadlines 21, 111
dealer 175
dealing 17, 114
deceitful 113
decide 183
deciding 120
decision 5, 74, 77-79, 82, 129, 192, 223-224, 253-254
decisions 74-75, 78, 80-81, 87, 91, 94, 96, 131, 190, 193, 224, 227
decrease 186
dedicated 7
deeper 10
defective 245
defects 185
define 2, 27, 34, 41, 58, 63, 81, 149, 177
defined 10, 15, 18, 25, 27-31, 33, 36, 38-39, 41, 43, 57, 65, 69, 73, 89, 102, 152, 156, 160, 174, 191-193, 207, 212, 216, 237, 251
defines 24, 32-33, 167, 177
defining 7, 112, 132, 150
definite 99, 160
definition 16, 19, 33, 36-37, 151, 169, 175, 181, 194, 201
degree 231-233, 239-240
delaying 52
delays 44, 171
delegate 230
delegated 32, 245
deletions 98
deliver 25, 36, 79, 116, 179, 227, 230
delivered 50, 117, 174, 251, 258
delivers 167
delivery 19, 115, 120, 245, 257, 259
demand 102, 201-202
demands 232, 239
demine 140
department 7, 124, 190, 217, 253
depend 218
dependent 120, 135

depends 120
deploy 97, 117
deployed 92
deployment 49
derive 95
Describe 16, 140, 146, 162-163, 169, 177, 247-248
described 1, 155, 222, 253
describing 30
deserving 218
design 1, 9, 63, 80, 87, 97, 123, 183, 201, 204, 242
designed 7, 9, 61, 80, 84, 86
designing 7
desired 24, 40, 62, 87, 167, 221, 244
detail 53, 79, 149, 153-154, 161, 172
detailed 64, 66, 140, 207, 242, 253
details 49
detect 93
determine 9, 108, 111, 130, 158, 170, 180
determined 63, 108, 140, 204
determines 108, 177-178
detracting 107
develop 73, 77-78, 83, 86-87, 138, 142, 152, 231
developed 9, 32, 34, 38, 76, 87, 143, 148, 150-151, 163, 182, 184, 187, 194, 211, 214, 222, 233, 243, 245
developing 62, 136, 154, 173
device 233
devices 226
diagram 3, 45, 64, 164
diagrams 49
dictates 173
Dictionary 3, 154-155
differ 170, 174
difference 148, 215
different 7, 22, 30, 37-39, 59, 64, 108, 115, 121, 136, 156, 169, 197, 211, 215, 224, 251, 253
difficult 62, 160, 165, 168, 177, 182
difficulty 216
dilemma 122
dimensions 25
direct 154, 189
direction 35, 43, 139
directly 1, 59, 61, 126
directors 120, 125

Directory 5, 227
Disagree 10, 15, 27, 43, 57, 73, 89, 102
disaster 44, 51
disclosure 92
discussion 123
displayed 40, 62, 158, 171
disputes 231, 256
disqualify 69
divergent 137
Divided 26, 32, 42, 56, 71, 88, 100, 127
document 9, 40, 131, 138, 151, 223-224
documented 40, 81, 84, 89-90, 93, 141, 149, 151, 176, 191-192, 207, 212, 216, 219-220, 225, 237, 241, 249, 251
documents 7, 155-156, 194, 211, 230, 253-255
dollar 241
dollars 189
domains 77
drawbacks 190
drawing 254
Driver 67
drivers 48, 66
drives 46
driving 122, 125
Duration 3, 137, 152, 169, 171
durations 34, 170
during 35, 75, 130, 139, 161, 166, 198, 201, 204-205, 209, 212, 224, 261
duties 190, 254
dynamic 53
dynamics 33
earlier 109
earliest 143
earned 5, 154, 170, 243-244
easily 149
economic 254
economical 119, 138
economy 76
eDiscovery 223
edition 8
editorial 1
educate 252
education 93
effect 140, 199

effective		16, 19, 103, 105, 111, 125, 171, 224-226, 246, 254, 261
effects 130, 134-135, 162, 195, 199, 228
efficiency		59, 90
efficient		79, 218, 254
effort	32, 49, 121, 155, 189, 234, 237
efforts	35, 77, 131, 134, 141, 225
either	160
Electrical		151
electronic		1, 209
element		241-242
elements		9, 39, 70, 108, 188, 227, 242, 253
elicit	187
e-mail	144
embarking		29
emergent		53
emerging		65, 99
emotions		121
employed		194
employee		107, 116, 183, 247
employees		18, 22, 24, 60, 106-107, 120, 177
employer		245
employers		133
empower		7
empowered		225
enable 260
enablers		112
enabling		225
encourage		81, 93
encouraged		225
end-users		197, 245
engage		123, 195, 212, 229, 231, 239
engagement		44, 87, 133, 225
engine 233
Engineers		151
enhance		100, 232
enhanced		124
enhancing		90
enough		7, 69, 104, 115, 120, 129, 146, 233, 237
ensure 34, 40, 63, 66, 80, 103, 111, 113, 117, 121, 137, 150, 183, 187, 193, 210, 228, 230, 232, 239
ensures		117
ensuring		9, 104, 136, 243

entail 56
entered   149
Enterprise   218
entire 241
entities 44
entity 1
equally 258
equipment   18-19, 245-246
equipped   39
equitably   32, 232
errors   103, 245
escalated   130, 216
essential   76, 177, 232
essentials   105, 214
establish   73, 97, 179
estimate   51, 54-55, 148, 156, 169, 171, 249
estimated   28, 36, 45, 51, 110, 138, 177, 179, 200, 246-248
estimates   3-4, 39, 54, 71, 136, 154, 169, 177, 181-182
estimating   3-4, 157, 171, 179-180, 207-208
estimation   86, 136-137, 141, 194
etcetera   55, 115
ethical 25, 106, 114, 249
ethics   201
ethnic 124
evaluate   77, 82, 149
evaluated   129, 255
evaluating   83, 87
evaluation   65, 74, 79, 138, 185, 209-210, 231, 254
evaluative   215
evaluators   209
events 19, 75, 87, 242
everyday   60
everyone   32
everything   223
evidence   10, 47, 218, 226, 254
evolution   43
evolve 96
examined   41
example   2, 8, 12, 19, 64, 99, 151
examples   7-8
exceed   152, 173
exceeding   44
excellence   7

excellent 53
excess 241
exchange 239
exclude 80
excluded 154
execute 129, 237, 250
executed 222
Executing 5, 215
execution 97, 138, 150
executive 7, 119
executives 104
exempt 245
exercise 25
existence 202, 205
existing 9, 94, 99, 105, 148
exists 164
expect 104, 143, 171, 204
expected 23, 34, 82, 103, 113, 139, 170, 223, 237
expecting 259
expense 241
expenses 229-230
experience 28, 117, 122-123, 201, 204, 247
experiment 126
expert 169
expertise 175, 177, 190, 201, 246
experts 40
expiration 164
explained 9
explicitly 106
explore 64, 202, 232
exposures 86
expressed 138
extent 10, 18, 21, 33, 137, 154, 220, 233, 241, 246
external 35, 113, 141, 185, 195
facilitate 10, 19, 61, 98, 209, 239
facilities 144, 210
facing 23, 122, 199
factors 49, 84, 107, 179, 203
failed 55
failure 48, 105, 119, 134
fairly 32
familiar 8
families 177

fashion 1, 29
feasible		54, 58, 103, 157, 179
feature 9
features		138, 249
feedback		29, 33, 55, 129
filter	185
finalized		12
financial		44, 62, 68, 71, 183, 237, 253-254
fingertips		9
finish	143, 158, 160, 164, 243
focused		53
follow	90, 108, 115, 165, 237
followed		29, 140, 157, 209, 211, 261
followers		121
following		8, 10, 188
for--and		90
forecast		244
forefront		111
foresee		162
forget	9
formal	6, 105, 143, 183, 193, 208, 240, 249-250, 261
formally		31, 202, 241
format 9, 219, 228
formats		156, 234
formula		11, 114
Formulate		27
forward		125
foster	105, 119
framework		97, 117, 188
freaky	115
frequency		29, 96, 108, 181
frequent		157
frequently		51, 56, 232-233
friend	105, 109, 122
friends 177
frontiers		82
fulfill	103, 130
full-scale		87
fulltime 194
function		219, 250
functional		138, 155
functions		38, 110-111, 144-145, 148, 167, 192, 220, 227, 240
funded 253

278

funding   104, 114, 238-239, 253-254, 260
further 199
future   7, 49, 91, 100, 122, 154, 202-203
gained 59, 91, 99
gather 10, 27, 29-30, 34, 36-37, 43, 58, 66, 71, 184
gathered   33, 63-64, 67, 69, 71
gathering   31-32, 38, 145
General   131, 249
generally   218, 242
generate   61, 70, 186, 246
generated   64, 154
generation   8, 66
generators   203, 246
getting 54, 140, 223
global 76, 118, 162
govern 103, 239, 246
governance   25, 105, 141, 176, 191
governing   254
graded   219
graphical   174
graphics   22
graphs 8
greatest   75, 225
ground 68
grounded   253
grouped   160
groups 108, 141, 157, 184, 193, 211-214, 217, 225, 239, 260
growth 62, 107, 162, 261
guarantee   79
guaranteed   31
guidance   1
guidelines   138, 223
guides 138
habits   106
handle 166, 202, 204-205
handled   210, 254
happen   21, 124, 200, 205
happened   139
happening   118
happens   7, 41, 45, 55, 104, 106-107, 140-141, 180, 199-200, 205, 256
hardest   51
hardly   244

hardware   151, 215-216
havent 102
Having 199
hazards   205, 246
health 110
hearing   124
helpdesk   219
helping   7, 149
hidden 55
highest 22
high-level   27, 30
highlight   192
Highly 60
high-tech   121
hijacking   125
hiring 98
historical   169, 180
history 158, 182, 260
hitters 61
hitting 243
honest 114
horizon 122
humans   7
hypotheses   57
identified   1, 21-23, 25, 37, 39, 64-65, 67, 71, 82, 85, 140, 154, 175-176, 185, 192, 205, 208, 212, 223, 227, 235, 241, 246, 253
identify 9-10, 16, 18, 64-66, 86, 149, 170, 180, 195, 213, 241
ignore 18
ignoring   104
imbedded   91
impact 4, 29, 44, 46, 49, 53-55, 73, 118, 130, 136-137, 177, 199-203, 215, 221-222, 228, 231, 235, 238, 246
impacted   50, 150, 213-214
impacting   173
impacts   50, 171
implement   25, 63, 89
implicit 110
important   18, 25, 39, 58-59, 61, 115, 119-120, 125-126, 131, 167, 252
improve   2, 9, 63, 73, 75-76, 79-85, 87, 129, 131, 183, 251-252, 258-260
improved   74, 76, 83, 91
improves   129

improving 78, 217
incentives 98
incidence 203
incident 224
include 24, 80, 142, 176, 208, 210
included 2, 7, 18, 145, 157, 172, 180, 219, 247-248, 257
INCLUDES 9
including 17, 31-33, 43, 59, 85, 94, 97, 150, 156, 202, 235, 246, 258
increase 114, 202-203
increased 104
increasing 114
incurred 53
incurrence 241
incurring 190
in-depth 8, 10
indicate 69, 95, 117
indicated 93
indicators 22, 47, 58-61, 83, 94, 241
indirect 49, 155, 190, 241
indirectly 1
individual 1, 55, 136, 156, 158, 174, 229, 254, 259
industry 89, 104, 112, 162, 225
infinite 118
influence 82, 125, 133-134, 191-192, 223
influences 103, 162, 235
informal 239
informed 115, 246
ingrained 100
inherent 109
in-house 131, 184
initial 27, 120
initially 35
initiated 179, 185, 221
Initiating 2, 113, 129
initiative 10, 187-188, 195
injuries 245
injury 246
Innovate 73
innovation 45, 59, 76, 119, 123
innovative 115, 136, 179, 215
in-process 58
inputs 30, 37, 51, 68, 98, 169-170

inside 22
insight 61, 65
insights 8
inspect 219
inspector 219
inspired 103
instead 120
Institute 151
instructed 142-143
integrate 74, 97, 106
integrated 210
integrity 22, 106, 222
intended 1, 86, 200
INTENT 15, 27, 43, 57, 73, 89, 102
intention 1
interact 111
interest 118, 185, 217, 260
interested 254, 259
interests 15, 196, 214
interim 111
internal 1, 35, 68, 105, 113, 150, 185, 195
interpret 10
interval 190
interview 114, 259
introduce 53, 201, 253
introduced 239
invest 64
investment 19, 51, 65, 87, 203-204
investor 55
invoice 227
involve 124, 134, 141
involved 18, 25, 31, 48, 59, 63, 121, 148, 157, 169, 184, 192-193, 195, 201, 207, 211-212, 217, 232, 234, 245, 254, 257
involves 95
issues 16-19, 21, 130-131, 144, 148-149, 151, 156, 166, 173, 216, 226, 230, 235, 246, 260
istoppers 200
itself 1, 23
joining 148
jointly 231, 239
judgment 1, 169
justified 98
killer 115

knock-on 199
knowledge 9, 28, 35, 59, 83, 91, 93, 98-100, 105, 108-109, 117, 169, 213, 257
lacked 89
largely 64
latest 8
leader 16, 60, 70, 83, 230
leaders 32, 68, 71, 96, 117, 121-122, 231, 235
Leadership 1-13, 15-53, 55-56, 58-71, 73-88, 90-92, 94-98, 100, 102-134, 136-146, 148-150, 152-154, 156-160, 162, 164-177, 179-185, 187, 189-195, 197-199, 201-205, 207-209, 211-223, 225, 227-231, 233, 235, 237-241, 243-247, 249-253, 256-258, 260-261
learned 6, 91, 94, 116, 188, 193, 250-251, 258, 260
learning 100, 154, 224
lesson 258
lessons 6, 87, 91, 116, 188, 193, 250, 260
letter 144
levels 17, 22, 39, 59, 61, 83, 87, 89, 91, 110, 152, 183, 241
leverage 38, 76, 91, 122, 171, 180
leveraged 35
levers 213
liability 1
licensed 1
lifecycle 54, 68
Lifetime 9
likelihood 84, 86, 203
likely 83, 97, 105, 134, 199, 202-203, 209, 223, 226
limitation 50
limited 9, 191
linked 42, 144, 223
listed 1, 188
listen 113, 126
locally 76, 176
located 176
location 224, 229
logged 176
logical 166
logically 156
longer 97, 201
long-term 91, 109, 118
looking 237
losing 54
losses 21, 28

machines 216
magnitude 81
maintain 89, 106-107, 253
maintained 79, 240
makers 74, 98, 129
making 16, 77, 80, 82, 122, 187-188, 192, 260
manage 33, 36, 46, 54, 63, 79, 85, 87-88, 108, 119, 130-131, 138-139, 142, 146-147, 182, 187, 189, 198, 200, 236, 241
manageable 42, 81
managed 7, 39, 60, 67, 69, 79, 81, 83, 87, 92, 97, 176, 250
management 1, 3-5, 8-9, 19, 22, 25, 31, 33, 48, 59-60, 64, 70-71, 73-74, 76, 78, 83-85, 103, 105, 108, 110, 122, 126, 134-135, 138-140, 142, 148-151, 154-156, 160, 167, 169, 173, 175-176, 183, 192-193, 195, 197, 201, 204, 207-208, 210-211, 213, 216, 218, 224-225, 227, 237-238, 241, 244-245, 249-252, 256, 258, 261
manager 7, 9, 25, 36, 40, 109, 138, 208, 212, 217, 249
managers 2, 128, 193, 202, 211
manages 76, 84, 247
managing 2, 84, 128, 133, 226
mandate 131
mandatory 221
manner 21, 80, 154, 189-190, 219-220, 226, 232, 249
mantle 104
Mapping 63, 67, 70
marked 149
market 16, 162-163, 243
marketer 7
marketing 144
markets 18
material 154, 185, 209-210
materials 1
matrices 146
Matrix 2-4, 134, 146, 189-190, 203
matter 40, 47, 232, 246
Maximize 203
meaningful 46, 126, 233, 241
measurable 28, 34, 131, 194
measure 2, 9, 22, 24, 31, 38, 43-45, 47-48, 50, 54-55, 59, 73, 76-77, 83, 86, 90, 92, 95, 99, 180-181, 185-186, 216
measured 19, 44, 47-48, 50, 52-53, 87, 93, 98, 206
measures 43-47, 51-52, 58-59, 61, 66, 83, 89, 94-95, 136, 183, 185, 199, 215, 219, 233, 260
measuring 90, 241

mechanical 1
mechanism 259
mechanisms 135
medical 226
medium 232, 243
meeting 29, 32, 99, 150, 156, 175, 196, 218, 223, 229-230, 259
meetings 28, 30-31, 36, 129, 149, 223
megatrends 120
Member 5, 40, 109-110, 217, 229, 233
members 29, 31-32, 40, 137, 140, 176, 194-195, 198, 207, 220, 227-233, 239-240, 254, 260
memorable 185, 233
memory 220
message 213-214
method 46, 136, 138, 148, 185, 195, 231-232, 246
methods 29, 54, 66, 138, 140, 150, 180, 183, 194, 201
metrics 4, 36, 66, 98, 132, 142, 182, 185-186
milestone 3, 141, 162, 181, 207, 212
milestones 33, 133, 160, 164, 194
minimize 136-137, 202
minimizing 68
minimum 247, 255
minority 15
minutes 29, 79, 156, 230
missed 124
missing 62, 121, 160
mission 58, 62, 119, 125, 131, 205, 240
mistakes 260
Mitigate 79, 136
mitigation 138-139, 201
mobile 233-234
modeling 65, 130
models 16, 65, 124
modern 141
modified 97
module 155
moment 124
moments 60
momentum 110, 124
monetary 22
monitor 90, 92, 94, 96, 99, 180
monitored 90-91, 97, 159, 176

monitoring 5, 90-91, 93-94, 98, 166, 173, 197, 237, 242
monthly 241
months 79, 81
motivate 118, 239
motivation 16, 95, 126
multiple 194, 197
narrow 67
national 254
nature 53, 155, 241
nearest 11
nearly 123
necessary 65, 67, 74, 113, 115, 124, 151, 180, 190, 197, 209, 215, 221, 225, 239, 253
needed 17, 19-23, 25, 37, 65, 68, 92, 100, 129, 171, 211, 213, 215, 237
negative 119, 134, 213
negatively 215
negotiate 113
negotiated 120
neither 1
network 3, 164, 239-240
Neutral 10, 15, 27, 43, 57, 73, 89, 102
normal 100, 215
Notice 1
notified 256
notify 229
number 26, 42, 45, 56, 71, 88, 100, 127, 185, 204, 246, 262
numbers 125, 230
numerous 256
objection 23
objective 7, 45, 132, 135, 149, 178, 201, 223, 242
objectives 17, 20, 25, 27, 31, 42, 58, 62, 95, 97, 105, 117, 125, 130, 138, 145, 175-176, 181, 200, 206, 218, 226, 234-235
observe 191
observed 75
observing 150
obsolete 120
obstacles 23, 162, 179
obtain 113, 250
obtained 33, 151
obtaining 51
obviously 10
occurring 75, 203

occurs 17, 51, 100, 251-252
offerings 61, 84
offers 210
office 175, 184, 209, 218, 256
officials 256
offshore 144
one-time 7
ongoing 98, 159, 225
opened 242
operate 220
operates 112
operating 5, 53, 95, 220, 229
operation 92, 171
operations 9, 90, 97, 100
operators 90, 254
opinion 226
opinions 202
opponent 223
opponents 236
opposite 105, 112
opposition 114
optimal 73, 78, 80, 210, 247
optimize 82, 90
optimized 113
option 109
options 25, 199
ordering 254
orient 99
origin 144
original 181, 208, 223
originally 156
originate 98
others 130, 173, 179, 181, 195, 203, 224, 231, 245-246, 252
otherwise 1
outcome 10, 79, 167, 228
outcomes 80, 85, 90, 124, 134, 179, 200, 244-245, 251-252
outlier 160
outlined 95
output 38, 57-59, 62, 64-65, 67, 69, 93, 95
outputs 30, 63, 66, 68-69, 98, 134, 166
outside 81, 129
Outsource 69, 257
outweigh 45, 197

overall 9-10, 20, 56, 97, 108, 110, 130, 145, 150, 164, 223, 247, 252
overcome 179
overhead 154-155, 241-242
overheads 175
overlooked 177, 215, 251
oversees 129
oversight 70, 157, 175, 184, 234, 245
overtime 160
owners 152
ownership 28, 93
package 155, 242
paradigms 122
paragraph 106
parameters 97
Pareto 61
particular 64, 237
Parties 86, 254, 256-257
partners 25, 31, 86, 93, 107, 117, 120, 137, 162, 232, 237
pattern 203
patterns 77
paycheck 111
paying 120
payment 256
payments 207, 253-254
payroll 245
pending 222
people 7, 21, 46, 53, 59, 86, 93-94, 104, 106-107, 110-111, 115, 122, 124, 126, 129, 189, 196-197, 204, 218, 229, 237, 243, 260
perceived 232
percent 109
percentage 146
perception 76, 83, 114
perform 21, 29, 32, 37, 139, 142, 157-158, 167, 253-254
performed 146, 158-159, 189, 197, 227, 242
performing 200, 210
perhaps 24, 243
period 80, 154
periodic 207
periods 253
permission 1
permit 53
person 1, 134, 190

personal 125, 260
personally 146
personnel 20, 22, 68, 90, 175, 187-188, 202, 2C8
pertinent 90
phased 154
phases 54, 82, 136, 160, 198
pitfalls 109
placed 190
planet 94
planned 95, 97, 154, 158, 170-171, 189, 199, 241, 251, 259
planners 98
planning 3, 8, 100, 130, 136, 143, 148, 155, 165-167, 201, 217, 225, 251
platform 233-234
players 77
pocket 179
pockets 180
points 26, 42, 56, 67, 71, 88, 100, 127, 187
policies 138, 214, 254
policy 31, 98, 141, 166, 176, 200, 253
political 42, 111, 202
population 137
portfolio 115, 215, 238
portfolios 195
portray 61
positioned 179
positive 81, 119, 124, 139, 213, 226
possess 246
possible 45, 55, 67, 70, 89, 109, 118, 239, 246
possibly 204
potential 16, 49, 69, 75, 82, 85, 87, 110, 120-121, 148, 197, 199-200, 205
practical 58, 73, 75, 89, 218
practice 121
practiced 112
practices 1, 9, 68, 77, 91, 98, 141, 234, 249
preach 121
precaution 1
precludes 210
predicting 90
prediction 160
predictive 167
preferred 259

pre-filled	8
prepare	188, 229
prepared	261
preparing	225
present	91, 112, 122, 211, 216, 233
presented	16, 228
presenting	230
preserve	30
preserved	63
prevent	140, 151, 209, 226
prevents	16
previous	35, 162, 247
previously	221
primary	51
principal	112
principals	86, 108
principles	138, 141
priorities	46, 48-50, 52, 181, 214
priority 51, 54
privacy	35
problem	15-16, 19-20, 24-25, 27, 32-35, 46, 48, 58-59, 143, 218, 243
problems	16, 18, 20, 23-25, 75, 78, 86, 94, 107, 136, 145, 186, 188
procedure	220, 229, 245, 254
procedures	9, 84, 89-90, 93, 95, 150, 166, 185, 187, 209, 214, 223, 241, 245, 254
proceed	154
proceeding	171
process	1-7, 9, 27, 29-30, 34, 37-38, 50, 58-61, 64-71, 75, 80, 91-93, 95, 98-100, 129-130, 136-137, 139-143, 146, 148-150, 156, 166, 169-170, 173, 178, 181, 183-184, 187-188, 193, 198, 201, 209, 215, 219, 224, 227, 232, 237, 243, 247, 249, 251, 253-254, 258, 261
processes	44, 56, 58-60, 62-63, 65, 68-69, 71, 97, 99, 129, 134, 140, 149-150, 202, 216, 222, 225, 237, 249, 251
produce	59, 166, 217, 227, 237
produced	67, 81, 237
producing	146
product	1, 51, 59, 61, 113, 115, 137, 148, 150, 162-163, 170, 173, 203, 205, 217-218, 221, 235, 243-246, 249, 251, 258, 261
production	34, 104

products 1, 15, 19, 53, 108, 117, 132, 136, 146, 215, 218, 221
profit 186
profits 181
program 17, 49, 64, 91, 129, 136-137, 183, 215, 225
programme 237
programs 195, 218, 225, 246
progress 41, 77, 97, 120, 122, 140, 180, 187-188
prohibit 253
project 2-8, 15-16, 21, 23, 32, 58, 68, 73, 95-97, 103-105, 109-111, 114, 119-120, 124, 126, 128-134, 136-146, 148-150, 152-153, 156-160, 162, 164-165, 167-184, 189-194, 198-199, 201-204, 207-208, 211-212, 214-218, 220-222, 227-228, 231, 235, 237-240, 243-244, 246-247, 249-252, 257-258, 260-261
projected 189
projects 2, 48, 109, 116-117, 128-129, 136, 146, 173, 193, 195, 197, 202-203, 211, 215, 217-218, 230, 243-244, 258
promising 115
promote 53, 106
promptly 130, 216
proofing 75
proper 92, 142, 190
properly 28, 32, 129, 145
property 226
proponents 236
proposal 142, 162
proposals 98, 209-210
proposed 25, 45, 55, 80, 86, 138, 142, 145, 156, 199, 247-248
protect 63, 115
protected 63
proved 249
provide 17, 65, 106, 111, 133, 144, 164, 170, 175, 177-179, 189, 231, 239
provided 11, 90, 183, 193, 260
providers 86
provides 167
providing 92, 133, 173, 181
provision 193, 223
public 135, 254
published 209
publisher 1
pulled 109
purchase 7, 209, 212

purpose	2, 9, 125, 180, 223, 229, 232-233, 239
purposes	154, 245
pushing	115
qualified	32, 58, 60, 69, 139, 170
qualifies	62, 69
qualify	50, 62, 70
quality	1, 4-5, 9, 23, 47-48, 55, 59, 62, 66, 68, 74, 89, 91, 123, 129, 140, 175-177, 183-188, 194, 207, 211, 215, 220, 223, 225, 245
quantified	98
quantify	50
quantities	210
quantity	209
question	10, 15, 27, 43, 57, 73, 89, 102, 119, 187
questions	7-8, 10, 58, 195, 215, 236
quickly	9, 60, 64, 71
ranking	220
rather	53, 114, 242, 245
rating	219
ratings	209
rational	154
rationale	211, 224
reached	24
reaching	105
readable	209
readiness	34, 207, 213
readings	90
realistic	24, 66, 105, 138, 197, 216
reality	157
realize	47, 233
realized	117
really	7, 39
reason	105, 110
reasonable	81, 102, 138, 150
reasons	29, 253
reassess	193
rebuild	115
recasts	178
receive	8-9, 36, 54, 209, 213, 261
received	41, 111, 253-254, 261
recently	119
recipient	21, 256
recognised	83
recognize	2, 15, 17-19, 22-23, 77-78

recognized   15-16, 18-19, 21-22, 24, 69, 239
recognizes   25
recommend   105, 122
record 183, 187
recording   1, 229
records   68, 123, 184, 189, 257
recovery   44, 151
recruiting   169
recurrence   205
redefine   24, 30
re-design   67
reduce 51, 53, 155, 224
reduced   205
reducing   99, 114
references   262
reflect 59, 91-92, 96, 183
reform 55, 98, 103, 123
reforms 25, 54-55
refuses 205
regard 137
regarding   108, 125, 184, 209, 217, 254
Register   2, 4, 133, 199
regret 77
regular 28, 41, 69, 175, 248
regularly   30-31, 40, 129
regulation   203
regulatory   16
reimbursed   230
reject 149
rejected   140, 253
rejecting   140
relate 71, 169, 222
related 16, 69, 96, 129, 183, 195, 244
relation   18, 24, 125
relations   113
relative 97
relatively   105
release 156, 193-194, 211
releases   247
relevant   34, 44, 65, 97, 103, 150, 240, 254
reliable 39, 205
remain 29
remaining   180

293

rephrased 9
replace 50
replicated 258
Report 5-6, 74, 90, 140, 217, 239, 247, 253
reported 154, 185, 244
reporting 60, 100, 110, 156, 169, 245
reports 54, 92, 133, 183
repository 156, 194, 211
represent 87, 221
reproduced 1
request 5, 58, 143, 176, 181, 219-222
requested 1, 80, 210, 221
requests 176, 203, 209, 219
require 40, 60, 67, 97, 99, 166, 173, 201, 239
required 18-19, 28, 34, 36, 39, 41, 49, 64, 68, 77, 82, 89, 130, 145, 151, 159, 161, 164, 171, 187, 216, 225, 230, 245, 258, 260
requires 209
requiring 133, 256
research 16, 110, 115, 169, 233
resemble 215
reserve 154
reserved 1
reside 81, 178
resolution 65, 87
resolve 18-19, 228, 231
resolved 130, 173, 216, 235
resource 3-4, 117, 129, 137, 160, 166-167, 193, 208, 213, 217, 229
resources 2, 7, 17, 19, 21, 38-40, 52, 62, 77, 85, 89, 94, 96, 104, 117-118, 122, 135, 144, 156, 159-161, 164, 167-168, 170-171, 180, 183, 189, 193, 227, 237-238, 258, 260
respect 1
respective 136
respond 199, 213, 245
responded 11
responding 199
response 16-17, 91-93, 95, 99, 213, 247
responses 85, 119, 199
responsive 179
result 65, 81, 87, 137, 148, 179, 221, 232, 256, 258
resulted 96
resulting 68, 149

results 8, 34, 36, 61, 73-74, 78, 82-86, 90, 94, 136, 169-170, 179, 187, 215, 237, 242
Retain 102
retained   61
retention   46, 169
retrospect   109
return 81, 164, 203
revenue   21, 43
revenues   51
review 9, 34, 59, 131, 184, 223, 225
reviewed   34, 148
Reviewer   232-233
reviews 164, 183, 207, 242
revised 71, 96
revisions   256
reward 53, 55, 70, 218
rewarded   22
rewards   98
rework 54-55
rights 1
robustness   162
routine 94, 241
rushing 196
safely 205
safety 117, 230, 246
salvaged   226
sampling   183
satisfied   121, 178, 227, 249
satisfies 243
satisfying   123
savings 39, 47, 55, 71
scalable   76
scenario   28, 35, 216
schedule   3-4, 41, 44, 85, 97, 111, 141, 144, 156-157, 164-165, 173-174, 176, 181, 193, 200, 207, 215, 221, 228, 241-242, 247, 258
scheduled   129, 143
schedules   157, 165, 174, 200, 242
scheduling   154, 156, 207
scheme   99
science   61
scopes 149
Scorecard   2, 11-13

scorecards   98
Scores 13
scoring 9
second   11
section 11, 26, 42, 56, 71, 88, 100, 127
sector 243
secure 255
securing   44, 105
security   22, 65, 85, 96, 99, 133, 151, 222
segmented   39
segments   38, 108
select 97
selected   78, 138, 180, 210, 241
selecting   229
selection   5, 209-210, 232
sellers 1
selling 102, 224
senior 96, 110, 117, 126
sensitive   52
sequence   159
sequenced   156
sequencing   103
series 10
servant 120
servers 216
service 1-2, 7, 51, 76, 83, 86, 89, 115, 131, 148, 162-163, 200, 209, 217-218, 261
services   1, 40, 53, 106, 108, 111, 177, 215, 230, 245, 247-248, 250, 256
session 143
setbacks   60, 71
setting 105, 107
several 59, 253
severely   67
severity   200
shared 99, 179, 224, 230
sharing 83, 100, 141
sheets 142
shifts   21
short-term   203

should 7, 18-19, 21, 24, 27, 30, 33, 48-49, 54, 60-61, 64, 79-80, 87, 90, 96, 105, 110, 112, 115, 117, 122, 126, 130-131, 133, 135-138, 142, 150, 155, 159, 167, 178, 182, 188, 199, 202-204, 206, 210, 219, 221, 228, 233, 241, 261
signature 121
signatures 166
signers 256
signing 183
similar 32, 35, 61, 84, 158, 182, 202
simple 105, 243
simply 8, 224
single 106, 230, 242, 253
single-use 7
situation 17, 43, 173, 178, 199, 243
situations 96, 103
skills 17-18, 69, 105, 109, 115, 125, 213, 216, 231-232, 238-239, 254, 260
smallest 20, 81
social 135
societal 103
software 19, 136, 141, 150, 202, 210, 215-216, 247
solicit 29
soliciting 230
solution 43, 58, 65, 73-76, 78, 80, 82, 85-87 89, 206, 237, 247-248
solutions 76, 79, 81-82, 87, 100, 202
solved 24
Someone 7
someones 232
something 123, 155, 197, 226
source 5, 114, 123, 150, 178, 205, 209-210
sources 34, 61, 64
special 28, 90, 131, 209, 214, 254
specific 8, 23, 28, 31, 34, 65, 115, 149, 151, 160, 162, 165-166, 168, 174, 177-178, 182, 191, 210, 213-214, 217, 222, 259
specified 105, 157, 251, 258
spoken 119
sponsor 25, 141, 176, 211, 228, 249
sponsors 25, 129, 187, 227
spread 95
staffed 40
staffing 17, 98, 138
stages 193, 254

standard   7, 89, 94, 166, 242, 247-248
standards   1, 9-10, 91-92, 98, 100, 129, 150-151, 185, 188, 222
started 8
starting 9
start-up   227
stated 106, 144, 183, 246, 251, 253-254, 260
statement   3, 10, 78, 86, 132, 140, 148, 151, 170
statements   11, 26, 33-34, 42, 56, 59, 71, 88, 100, 127, 149, 187
Status 5-6, 140, 193, 200, 211, 217, 241, 243-244, 247
steady 52
steering   157, 175, 184
stopper   145
storage   219
stored 226, 234, 255
stories 36
strategic   49, 77, 97, 125, 176, 245
strategies   80, 114, 123, 169, 201, 223-224, 226
strategy   20, 40, 52, 56, 83, 85, 94, 102, 108, 122, 200, 213, 223, 260
Stream 67, 70
strength   225
strengths   181, 249
stretch 107
strict   71
strive   107
striving 131
strong 191
Strongly   10, 15, 27, 43, 57, 73, 89, 102
structure   3, 49, 73, 85, 104-105, 137, 152, 167, 174, 210
Structured   112
structures   242
stubborn   113
stupid 113
Styles   1-6, 8-13, 15-53, 55-56, 58-71, 73-88, 90-92, 94-98, 100-134, 136-146, 148-150, 152-154, 156-160, 162, 164-185, 187, 189-195, 197-199, 201-205, 207-209, 211-223, 225, 227-231, 233, 235, 237-241, 243-247, 249-253, 256-258, 260-261
subdivide   155
subdivided   154
subject 8-9, 40
subjects   60
submitted   221
subsequent   210

subset 20
sub-teams   239
succeed   45, 120
success   24, 31, 33, 37, 41, 44, 47-48, 54, 77, 79, 84, 86, 93, 107, 114-115, 117, 119, 125-126, 134, 149, 183, 193, 197, 212, 218, 232, 252, 258
successes   114
successful   62, 80, 92, 103-104, 120, 167, 177, 196, 213, 217, 258
succession   92
sufficient   137, 220, 226, 237-238, 260
suggested   93, 221
suitable   203, 245-246
supervisor   191
supplier   84, 111, 175
suppliers   30, 57, 65, 117
supplies   250
supply 52, 162
support   7, 19, 74, 87, 92-93, 100, 111, 114, 126, 144, 166, 200, 202, 223, 226, 242, 247, 261
supported   66, 144, 198
supporters   134
supporting   82, 92, 187
supportive   141
supports   129
surface   94
surprise 135
surprised   261
SUSTAIN   2, 82, 102
sustaining   91
symptom   15, 47
system 9, 32, 58, 117, 122, 131, 144-145, 151, 167, 183-184, 189, 192, 222-223, 226, 234, 241, 243, 246, 254
systematic   45, 53
systems   53, 59, 68, 70-71, 79, 84, 97, 134, 225, 233, 244, 249
tackle 47
tactics 135, 223-224
takers 149
taking 43, 137, 218, 230, 242
talent 69, 110
talents 105
talking 7

tangle 189
target 37, 116, 137, 213-214
targets 107, 134, 194, 226, 243
tasked 93
technical   129, 144, 162, 201, 237
techniques   65, 124, 130, 156
technology   50, 83, 89, 115, 121, 162-163, 201, 209, 212, 229-230, 245
templates   7-8
tender 253, 255
tenders   253, 255
testable   32
tested 22, 130
testing 78, 87, 183-184, 201, 245
themes 233
themselves   53, 110, 231
theories   169
theory 95
therefore   205
therein 242
things 75, 111, 129, 197, 237, 251, 261
thinking   66, 81, 123
thinks   226
third-   86
thorough   74, 221
thought   229, 235
threat 22, 107
threatened   134
threats 140, 205
through   59, 69, 117, 149, 219, 224
throughout   1, 68, 123, 164
time-bound   34
timeframe   63, 160, 180
timeframes   18
timeline   150, 194, 221
timely 21, 29, 80, 190, 219-220
timetable   164
Timing 195, 228
together   115
tolerances   85
tolerated   158
tomorrow   94, 111
top-down   97

toward 99, 218
towards 65, 120
traced 181
tracked 141, 149, 175, 212, 219
tracking 35, 97, 148, 150, 174
trademark 1
trademarks 1
trained 32, 198, 202, 209
training 17, 21, 25, 64, 68, 77, 90, 93, 98, 213, 217, 225, 234, 254, 260
trainings 22
Transfer 11, 26, 42, 56, 71, 88, 93, 98, 100, 127, 213, 247
transition 116
translated 28
trends 59, 61, 65, 83, 139, 183
trigger 85
triggers 74, 175
trophy 104
trouble 112
trying 7, 111, 125, 185, 206, 226
turnaround 160
typical 216, 235
ubiquitous 118
ultimate 125
unclear 36
uncovered 145
underlying 77, 154
undermine 111
understand 40, 60, 86, 129, 142, 191, 231
understood 81, 84, 111, 145, 226, 232
undertake 60
underway 80
uninformed 115
uniquely 235
Unless 7
unresolved 166, 207
updated 8-9, 59, 157, 164, 207-208
updates 9, 98, 169, 248
updating 193
up-sell 126
up-to-date 253
urgency 201
usability 74, 106

useful 75, 91, 169
usefully 9, 20
utility 171
utilized 169, 233
utilizing 73
validate 47, 244
validated 27, 30, 34, 64, 69
Validation 243
Validity 144
valuable 7
values 96, 116-117
variables 70, 93
variance 5, 170, 231-232, 241
variances 155, 176, 242
variants 255
variation 15, 34, 61, 64, 99
variety 86
various 193, 254
vendor 76, 129, 164, 175
vendors 15, 86
verified 9, 27, 30, 34, 64
verify 44, 46-49, 51-54, 56, 90-91, 95, 148, 181, 234, 243, 253, 257
verifying 48, 51, 56
Version 247, 262
versions 30, 37
versus 230, 254
vested 118
vetting 151
viable 100, 153
vice-versa 259
violated 150
violations 151
virtual 234
vision 117, 139
visions 137
visual 185
visualize 158, 171
voices 133
volatile 76
volatility 201
volunteers 229
warranty 1

weaknesses   140, 249
website   219
wellbeing   183
whether   7, 95, 120, 258
-which 201
wholesaler   175
widespread   94
widgets   181
willing 186
window   160
within 60, 80, 154-155, 159, 190, 192, 212, 217, 221, 229, 249
without1, 11, 107, 115, 173, 221, 245, 256
workdays   200
worked   203, 207, 216, 261
workers   124
workflow   63, 223
workforce   17, 83, 108, 117, 123
working   95, 97, 183, 192, 197, 201, 223
Worksheet   3-4, 171, 179
worst-case   28
writing 141, 147
written 1
yesterday   17
youhave   143, 173
yourself   105, 109, 125

Printed in Great Britain
by Amazon